For Reavley & Audrey Osw...
To the learned gentleman and
his lady.
All Best Wishes _Dan Stewart_

Jan 11 '86

66 Any interference with nature is
damnable. Not only nature but
also the people will suffer. 99

Anahareo

The CANADIAN WILDLIFE ALMANAC

DARRYL STEWART

PUBLISHED BY LESTER & ORPEN DENNYS

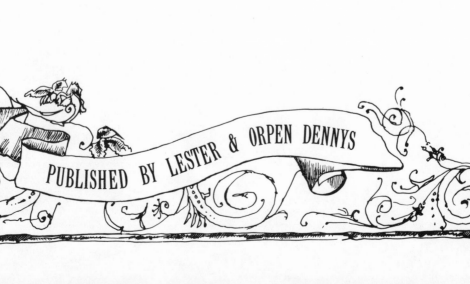

Canadian Cataloguing in Publication Data
Stewart, Darryl, date
The Canadian wildlife almanac

ISBN 0-919630-68-5
1. Natural history – Canada – Dictionaries.
I. Title.
QH106.S73   574.971   C81-094753-6

Design
C. Wilson/Sunkisst Graphics
Production
Paula Chabanais Productions
Hand-rendered lettering
on cover and title page
N.R. Jackson

Dedication

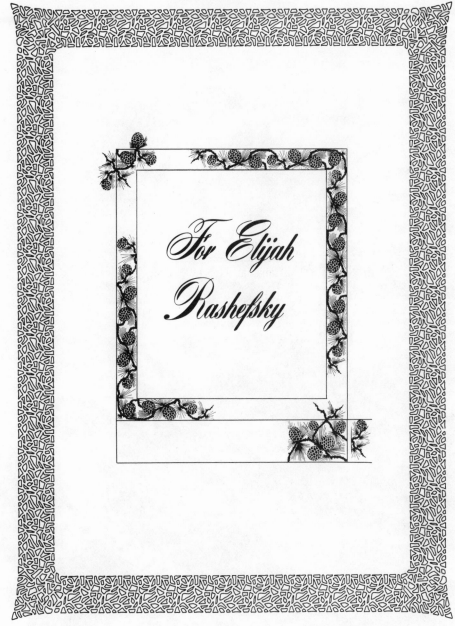

For Elijah
Rashefsky

The Fauna of Canada

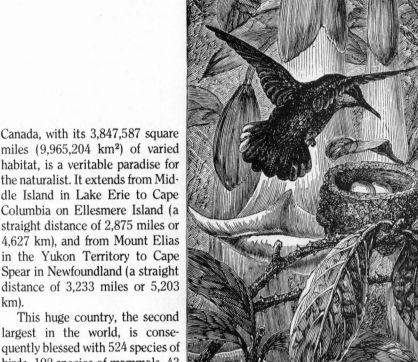

Canada, with its 3,847,587 square miles (9,965,204 km²) of varied habitat, is a veritable paradise for the naturalist. It extends from Middle Island in Lake Erie to Cape Columbia on Ellesmere Island (a straight distance of 2,875 miles or 4,627 km), and from Mount Elias in the Yukon Territory to Cape Spear in Newfoundland (a straight distance of 3,233 miles or 5,203 km).

This huge country, the second largest in the world, is consequently blessed with 524 species of birds, 192 species of mammals, 43 species of reptiles, 37 species of amphibians, and 182 species of freshwater fish.

Some of the world's largest animals inhabit this country of ours, as do some of the world's smallest. Characteristically Canadian mammals such as the Polar Bear (*Ursus maritimus*) and Grizzly Bear (*Ursus arctos horribilis*), two of the largest carnivores on earth, have their centre of abundance in Canada, as does the Moose (*Alces alces*), the largest of the deer, and the Wood Bison (*Bison bison athabascae*), our largest native land animal, which can weigh up to a ton (907 kg). Our smallest mammal is the Pygmy Shrew (*Microsorex hoyi*), which is found throughout Canada, and generally measures about three and one-half inches in length (89 mm), including the tail.

The White Pelican (*Pelecanus erythrorhynchos*), with a wingspread approaching ten feet (305 cm), is considered by many authorities to be the largest of all Canadian birds; while the Whooping Crane (*Grus americana*), at a height of five feet (152 cm), has the distinction of being our tallest. Our smallest native bird is the Calliope Hummingbird (*Stellula calliope*) from British Columbia, which rarely attains a length of more than two and three-quarter inches (70 mm).

There are 24 species (38 subspecies) of snakes that are native to Canada; the best-known and most widespread are the garter snakes. The Black Rat Snake (*Elaphe obsoleta obsoleta*) is Canada's largest species, and may attain a length of eight feet (244 cm), although on aver-

age it is usually smaller. It is confined, in this country, to parts of southern Ontario, where it feeds chiefly on mice and rats. The smallest native species is the Northern Red-bellied Snake (*Storeria occipitomaculata occipitomaculata*) which seldom exceeds twelve inches (30 cm) in length, and feeds chiefly on slugs, earthworms, and beetle larvae. It has a wide range in Canada, and is found from Saskatchewan to the Maritimes.

Canada's largest freshwater turtle is the somewhat prehistoric-looking Snapping Turtle (*Chelydra serpentina*), which is quite common. However, the animal is sadly maligned and frequently killed, and may become endangered before long. Our largest native salamander is the Mudpuppy (*Necturus maculosus*), which spends its entire life in the larval stage. It commonly grows to a length of eight to thirteen inches (203 to 330 mm), and there is on record a specimen having measured nineteen inches (483 mm).

The freshwater area of Canada constitutes 291,571 square miles (755,165 km²) and represents 7.6 per cent of the total area of the country. The largest freshwater lake totally confined within Canada is Great Bear Lake in the Northwest Territories, with an area of 12,000 square miles (31,080 km²).

The largest of our fish species is the

White Sturgeon (*Acipenser transmontans*), which not uncommonly attains a length of twenty feet (610 cm). The species is restricted to the far west of the continent, from the Aleutian Islands to Monterey, California. As much as 250 pounds (113 kg) of eggs may be found in a single female and marketed as caviar. The bulk of the commercial fishing of this species in Canada comes from the Fraser River. It is believed that the largest White Sturgeon ever reported was taken near Mission, British Columbia, and weighed over 1,800 pounds (817 kg).

Not all of Canada's wildlife originally evolved on this continent. A great many species, such as the Moose, Deer, Caribou (*Rangifer tarandus*), Bison (*Bison bison*), and Bighorn Sheep (*Ovis canadensis*), found their way from Asia to North America across the Bering land-bridge during the Pleistocene some 10,000 years ago. In fact, of North America's hoofed animals, only the Pronghorn (*Antilocapra americana*) is a true native. Conversely, mammals such as the horse and the camel, which were originally indigenous to North America, crossed over into Asia.

The opossum and the American Porcupine (*Erethizon dorsatum*), on the other hand, are known to have migrated here from the American tropics.

Many Canadian wildlife species are circumpolar in their distribution; that is, they are also to be found in the northern regions of the Old World. In fact, Canada's fauna far more closely resembles that of Europe than of the southern United States. To understand the reason for this it is necessary to remember that Asia and North America were once joined together by the Bering land-

bridge. Muskoxen (*Ovibos moschatus*) are found in Greenland as well as on Ellesmere Island, and Caribou are common in Lapland, where they are known as "Reindeer". The Moose is also native to the coniferous forests of Europe, and is known there as the "Elk". In no way should this animal be confused with the North American Elk (*Cervus canadensis*), which in actual fact is a Red Deer, and should properly be known by its original Indian name of "Wapiti". The Timber Wolf (*Canis lupus*), Grizzly Bear (*Ursus arctos horribilis*), Harbour Seal (*Phoca vitulina*), Ermine (*Mustela erminea*), and Red Fox (*Vulpes vulpes*) are just a few of the many Canadian mammals that are also represented in Europe by identical species.

The circumpolar birds include: the Snowy Owl (*Nyctea scandiaca*); Hawk Owl (*Surnia ulula*); Common Raven (*Corvus corax*); Northern Three-toed Woodpecker (*Picoides tridactylus*); Rock Ptarmigan (*Lagopus mutus*); Snow Bunting (*Plectrophenax nivalis*); Red Crossbill (*Loxia curvirostra*); Pine Grosbeak (*Pinicola enucleator*); and Hoary Redpoll (*Carduelis hornemanni*).

WAPITI

For many naturalists the first nature event of the year is the January Waterfowl Survey. This duck census, which was originated in 1947 by the Canadian Wildlife Service, is conducted along the Mississippi Flyway at strategic points in Ontario, Minnesota, Wisconsin, Kentucky, Arkansas, Tennessee, Louisiana, Mississippi, and Alabama. In Ontario, the count is usually held within the first ten days of January.

The purpose of the count is to try to determine duck, geese, and swan populations and distribution patterns along their migratory route, primarily as a guide to hunters. Although the practice has been discontinued in many areas, similar counts for Canada Geese are conducted during mid-November and mid-December, and other waterfowl surveys

DUCK COUNT

are carried out along the west coast and the Atlantic seaboard.

The most numerous overwintering waterfowl species in Ontario, according to these surveys, are: Canada Goose (*Branta canadensis*), Greater Scaup (*Aythya marila*), Mallard (*Anas platyrhynchos*), Oldsquaw (*Clangula hyemalis*), Common Goldeneye (*Bucephala clangula*), Common Merganser (*Mergus merganser*), and Black Duck (*Anas rubripes*).

Anyone wishing to take part in the January Waterfowl Survey should contact the Ontario Ministry of Natural Resources for information:
Ministry of Natural Resources,
Fish & Wildlife Branch,
Whitney Block,
Queen's Park,
Toronto, Ontario.
M7A 1W3 ᴖ

CALENDAR

2

Redshank (*Totanus sp.*) observed in Halifax County, Nova Scotia, 1960.

4

Allan Brooks, Canadian ornithologist, died, 1946.

8

William Pope, wildlife artist, born, 1811. Alfred Russel Wallace, British naturalist, born, 1823.

9

Christopher Columbus reported first **Manatee** (*Trichechus manatus*) sightings (Hispaniola), 1493.

Winter range of **Kirtland's Warbler** (*Dendroica kirtlandii*) discovered in the Bahamas, 1879.

2–10

January Waterfowl Survey (Mississippi Flyway).

16

Longest frog jump made by a **Sharp-nosed Frog** (*Rana oxyrhyncha*) — 32 feet, 3 inches (322 cm) (Cape Town, S. Africa).

17

Pygmy Sperm Whale (*Kogia breviceps*) recorded in Canada (dead specimen under the ice in Halifax Harbour, Nova Scotia), 1920.

27

John James Audubon died, 1851.

29

William Pope collection formally opened at the Toronto Public Library, 1917.

RED AND WHITE-WINGED CROSSBILLS

FEEDING BIRDS IN WINTER

When the snow lies thick on the ground and covers much of the birds' natural food, they must seek alternative sources of food elsewhere, often far from their natural habitat. At times like this, feeding stations can attract a great many birds, particularly if the operator of the station pays careful attention to the different requirements of birds.

CARDINAL

Some birds like seeds, others fruit. Sunflower seeds, suet, and peanuts (unsalted) are all popular foods and can be placed out to attract winter birds. The sunflower seeds are for grosbeaks, cardinals, and chickadees; the suet for woodpeckers and nuthatches; and the peanuts for blue jays.

BLACK-CAPPED CHICKADEE

Birds that come to feeders will generally accept a wide variety of foods. Most birds like bread crumbs, raisins, crushed pecans, and oatmeal as an additional supplement to their regular diet. Egg shells are especially valuable to female birds. The calcium contained in the shells helps to build up the shells of their own eggs. In addition, a receptacle filled with fresh water is an essential addition to the station.

It is important that you keep your feeding station clean at all times: birds

SNOW BUNTING

can get diseases from mouldy food. Throw out any leftover food from the previous day before putting out fresh food.

Once you begin to feed birds in the winter, it is important that you continue to do so throughout the entire season. Your birds may perish because they have become dependent on your station for food.

Bird feeders need not be elaborate to attract birds. For a backyard feeding station you need only a small feeding table with a roof for shelter. For a windowsill, a tray is adequate. Location is much more important than appearance. The feeders must be placed where the birds using them will be safe from cats and squirrels.

In many respects, the cold winter months are among the most interesting of the year for birdwatchers. It is during this period that some of the most gaudy perching birds come down from the north. The more regular winter visitors include the Evening Grosbeak (*Coc-*

cothraustes vespertina), Pine Grosbeak (*Pinicola enucleator*), Red Crossbill (*Loxia curvirostra*), White-winged Crossbill (*Loxia leucoptera*), Pine Siskin (*Spinus pinus pinus*), Common Redpoll (*Carduelis flammea*), Purple Finch (*Carpodacus purpureus*), Snow Bunting (*Plectrophenax nivalis*), and the Lapland Longspur (*Calcarius lapponicus*).

Apart from these visitors from the north, there are many resident winter species to be found within close proximity to your home. These resident species include: the Black-capped Chickadee (*Parus atricapillus*), White-breasted Nuthatch (*Sitta carolinensis*), Downy Woodpecker (*Picoides pubescens*), Hairy Woodpecker (*Picoides villosus*), Blue Jay (*Cyanocitta cristata*), Dark-eyed Junco (*Junco hyemalis*), Tree Sparrow (*Spizella arborea*), and perhaps the most beautiful of our winter residents, the Cardinal (*Cardinalis cardinalis*).

RED CROSSBILL

DOWNY WOODPECKER

A WINTER BIRD-BATH

To add to the attractiveness of your winter bird-feeding station you might consider providing drinking and bathing facilities for your winged visitors. Nature usually provides some open water in rapidly flowing streams, but in city areas birds may find difficulties in locating unfrozen water during severely cold periods.

The simplest way to provide this service is merely to set out a pan of warm water at the same time every day. Of course, after a few minutes on a really frosty day it will freeze over, and be of no further use. Some steady source of heat below it would prevent this from happening.

If a length of sewer-tile can be obtained, it makes a fine base for supporting a pan of water (such as a garbage-pail lid) and provides a protected space where a 100-watt light bulb can be suspended to provide the necessary heat to keep the water from freezing.

BLUE JAY

If a piece of tile is not readily available, another method that works well is to use a large ten- or twelve-inch (25 or 30 cm) clay flowerpot as a base on which to support the pan of water above the light. Instead of a garbage-pail cover, a large flowerpot saucer makes an excellent water tray. In any case, be sure to use a well-insulated, weather-proof extension cord to connect the light to an outdoor electrical outlet, so that short circuits and blown-out fuses will not result.

If a bird-bath can be set up on a wide outside window-ledge where a short cord can be used, so much the better, and when the birds have lost their initial fear, you will have an excellent chance for closeup observations of them when they come to drink and bathe.

➣ Oscar G. Rogers

GROUP OF SPARROWS

The Eastern Kingbird (*Tyrannus tyrannus*) is the lightweight champion of the bird colony. Though it is smaller than the Robin, the Kingbird thinks little of taking on an intruding Crow or Hawk and, in its finer moments, it will even attack an Eagle, hanging on to the Eagle's back while pulling out the feathers on its head and neck.

5

ONLY IN CANADA

The Vancouver Island Marmot (*Marmota vancouverensis*), a close relative of our familiar Groundhog (*Marmota monax*), is the only species of mammal whose entire population is found within the boundaries of Canada.

In fact, its habitat is entirely restricted to the alpine and sub-alpine regions of Vancouver Island, where no more than seventy individuals are believed to exist. On the basis of present knowledge it must be regarded as one of the world's rarest mammals.

It was discovered in 1910 on the peak of Mount Douglas, south of Alberni, by Harry Schlewald Swarth, a trapper who was working as a field collector for the University of California. He published his findings in 1911 but it was another twenty years before a sighting of the Vancouver Island Marmot was reported again. Since 1938 the only known colony has been the one on Forbidden Plateau.

The Vancouver Island Marmot has been formally designated an "endangered" species, and is currently afforded protection under the British Columbia Wildlife Act.

The greatest threat to its survival is being caused by advanced logging operations in the immediate environment of its

VANCOUVER ISLAND MARMOT

colony. Although the responsible companies have agreed to leave the timber immediately adjacent to the colony intact, the effect of any kind of disturbance on the marmot is unknown.

It would appear that our general lack of knowledge about this unique mammal and about the impact of human activities upon it is threatening its continued existence.

You can help to support the efforts to save this exclusively Canadian mammal by voicing your concern and writing to any or all of the following places:

Steven Rogers (MLA),
Ministry of the Environment,
Parliament Buildings,
Victoria, B.C.
V8V 1X5

D.J. Robinson,
Director of the B.C. Fish &
Wildlife Branch,
c/o Fish & Wildlife Branch,
1019 Wharf Street,
Victoria, B.C.
V8W 2Z3

D.M. Hebert,
Regional Wildlife Biologist
(Vancouver Island),
c/o Fish & Wildlife Branch,
324 Terminal Avenue,
Nanaimo, B.C.
V9R 5C8 ⌒

HERPTILES

A student of birds is called an ornithologist, of mammals a mammalogist, of insects an entomologist, and of reptiles a herpetologist, but there is no generally recognized name for one who works with amphibians — frogs, toads, and salamanders.

Up to now, the term "herpetology" has been used to cover both reptiles and amphibians, but as specialization increases it becomes more common to find herpetologists interested in reptiles who are not too well informed about amphibians, and vice versa. It is almost as if we used the same word to describe those who work with birds and with mammals. The word "amphibiologist" has been coined, but that is a rather awkward mouthful. Whether or not a new word comes into use to describe these

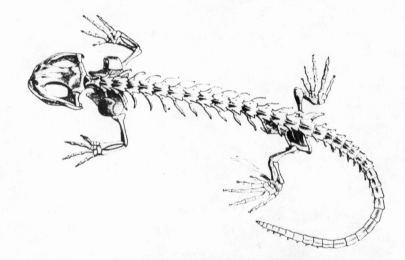

SKELETON OF A SALAMANDER

two branches of natural science, the herpetologists have invented a word to cover both their interests.

The word "herptile" is now coming into general use and, although it cannot as yet be found in most dictionaries, may well be before very long. A herptile may be a snake, a turtle, a lizard, a frog, a toad, or a salamander. An interesting fact about herptiles is that they never stop growing; if they lived long enough they would all become monsters. ⌒

BIRD MIGRATION AND CONTINENTAL DRIFT

The subject of bird migration is without doubt a perplexing one, and many theories have been put forward to try to explain this amazing phenomenon. It would appear that food is the driving force behind migration of birds, and their need to raise their young where there is a plentiful supply. A good definition might be that it is a form of adaptation that birds adopt in order to adjust to the changing demands of the seasons.

It is clear that migration has been in progress since earlier times, and it has been popular to relate its origins to the Pleistocene ice ages. One theory holds that migratory birds originally evolved in the more northern regions but retreated from there with the coming of the ice, only to move northward again as land became available. If this theory is correct then the yearly migration as we know it is simply a repetition of what has occurred for over tens of thousands of years since the glaciation. An alternative theory states that birds evolved not in the temperate zones but in the tropics, and that their movement north is but a repetition of their original period of colonization prior to the ice ages.

The question of continental drift as a possible factor in the origin of bird migration would appear to be quite reasonable, and was proposed as a theory as long ago as the 1940s. Certainly, the understanding of continental drift has satisfactorily answered some questions about why birds yearly travel such long distances.

The Arctic Tern (*Sterna paradisaea*) embarks each year on the longest migratory journey of any bird, as it travels a round-trip distance from the Arctic to the Antarctic oceans of about 22,000

ARCTIC TERN

GROUP OF GULLS AND TERNS

miles (35,406 km). This bird follows a most unusual path as it flies east across the North Atlantic, then south along the west coasts of Europe and Africa to Antarctica. The reason for all that unnecessary distance might well be explained in what an early proponent of the continental-drift theory described as migration "in accord with the pattern of the drift".

Formerly all land masses of the earth were composed of two subcontinents, known as Laurasia (in the north) and Gondwanaland (in the south). In keeping with the drift theory, the Arctic Tern's flight across the North Atlantic represents the east-west drift of the parts of Laurasia, and is thus a natural route for this bird to take as it reproduces the same flight pattern it has always done even before the separation and drifting apart of the two subcontinents. ༄

7

A PLURALITY OF BIRDS

Over the years we have coined a host of special terms to describe birds in groups. Here are some of these collective terms that still survive in English usage:

a gaggle of geese

a siege of herons or bitterns

a plump of waterfowl

a skein of geese (flying)

a herd of swans, cranes, or curlews

a badelyng of ducks

a sord (or sute) of mallards

a spring of teal

a company of wigeons

a cast of hawks

a bevy of quail

a covey of partridges

a chattering of choughs

a host of sparrows

a muster of peacocks

a nye of pheasants

COMMON PHEASANT

a covert of coots

a brood of chickens

a congregation of plovers

a desert of lapwings

a wisp (or walk) of snipe

a fall of woodcock

a bazaar of murres

a flight of doves or swallows

an exaltation of larks

a watch of nightingales

a building of rooks

a murder of crows

a charm of finches

a descent of woodpeckers

a murmuration of starlings

a parliament of owls

SNOWY OWL

OF ANCIENT LINEAGE

In one form or another fish have existed on earth for nearly 300 million years. Except for some tropical species like the Lung Fish (*Polypterus sp.*) and the Climbing Perch (*Anabus testudinosus*), they have never adapted themselves to any form of land living. Like snakes, they have neither eyelids or ears; they receive sound as vibrations transmitted along a lateral nerve which is plainly discernible on a Speckled Trout (*Salvelinus fontinalis*). Fish have a fairly well-developed sense of taste and can communicate with their own kind by grunts, squeals, and other sounds that have been picked up and classified by sonar. A boated Lake Trout (*Salvelinus namaycush*) will utter a recognizable sound of fright. The ages of scaled fish can be determined by the number of rings, like trees. In scaleless fish, such as sturgeon and catfish, biologists can determine ages by examining the skull structures at the point where the ears would be if there were any.

Fish are largely cannibalistic and therefore have a high mortality rate. No more than one in one hundred of the eggs laid by an adult fish reaches maturity. A large female Carp (*Cyprinus carpio*) may spawn 300,000 eggs, a Lake Trout almost as many, and other smaller fish proportionally as many. Because fish spawn at different times, large numbers of the eggs are devoured by other fish before they hatch or soon afterwards. Even the parents show no compunction about swallowing their young. Their interest ends when they have herded their progeny into shallow water. Harsh as this may seem, it is all a part of the laws of nature, laws which man often violates even with the best of intentions. ⌒

The Common Mackerel (*Scomber scombrus*) is a fish with a major problem — it can never sit still. Unlike most fish, it has no air bladder and therefore cannot suspend itself motionless in the water. If it stayed still it would sink to a depth at which the pressure would crush it. The Mackerel must keep swimming on constantly to save itself: in other words, it must keep running to stay in the same place.

PIT VIPERS

The rattlesnake is a member of a group of venomous snakes known as "Pit Vipers", so called because of two small pits located in the head between the nostril and the eye.

The function of these pits was unknown until Dr. G.K. Noble of the American Museum of Natural History discovered that they were sensory areas that detect heat and cold. During a series of experiments he plugged the nostrils of a rattlesnake with cotton soaked in collodin and applied adhesive tape to its eyes. He then placed an electric light bulb near the reptile's head. The snake struck unerringly at the bulb even though it could neither see nor smell it. If one of the pits was plugged, the snake would not strike at the bulb on that side of its head but would hit it if the warm globe was held at that side of its head where the pit was open. The snake made no attempt to strike when both pits were sealed up.

The rattle on the end of the tail of the rattlesnake is used as a warning signal to ward off the attentions of would-be predators. Contrary to popular belief the age of a snake cannot be determined by counting the number of rattles on its tail; a snake may produce several rattles in the course of a year and these may be broken off during its travels through rocky areas.

The fangs of a venomous snake work in a manner similar to a hypodermic needle: the poison is drained out through the tubelike points. When the fangs are not in use they are folded back against the roof of the snake's mouth. ⌒

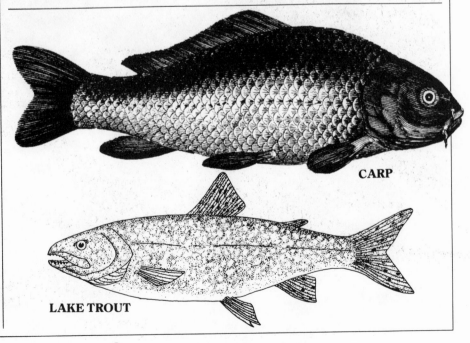

CARP

LAKE TROUT

FOXES

FEBRUARY

Popular superstition of unknown origin has it that the Groundhog (*Marmota monax*), or Woodchuck, arises from its winter torpor on February 2nd. It comes to the surface and if it then sees its shadow on the snow, it retires for another six weeks' slumber. If no shadow is visible, it continues more or less actively above ground until spring. Convincing statistical evidence, however, does not support this tradition.

It is true that among ground animals, the Groundhog awakens earlier than most, sometimes as early as the first week in February. And it is also true that, having looked about, it may go back to its den again, but probably not for long and certainly not to sleep for any specific period. The animal is rather unaccountably erratic in the matter of hibernation; it seems often to retire for the season while the sun still casts considerable warmth,

GROUNDHOG DAY

and to push its way to the surface while the ground is still buried under several feet of snow.

Although of short duration, the torpor of the animal is quite profound. Renowned nineteenth-century naturalists John James Audubon and John Bachman tell of a Groundhog in captivity aroused after six weeks' slumber, only with the greatest of difficulty, by being placed by an open fire; when the source of the heat was removed, it quickly curled up into a ball.

The North American legend of Groundhog Day is considered to be a variation on the traditional belief which sometimes includes the bear or Badger (*Meles meles*), and is associated with Candlemas (also February 2nd) in England. According to an old English song:

If Candlemas be fair and bright,
Come, Winter, have another flight;
If Candlemas bring clouds and rain,
Go, Winter, and come not again. ❧

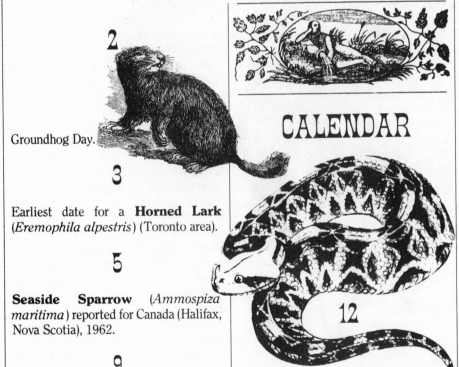

CALENDAR

2

Groundhog Day.

3

Earliest date for a **Horned Lark** (*Eremophila alpestris*) (Toronto area).

5

Seaside Sparrow (*Ammospiza maritima*) reported for Canada (Halifax, Nova Scotia), 1962.

9

Longest-lived Ape, an **Orangutan**, "Guas", died at age 57 in the Philadelphia Zoological Gardens, 1977.

12

Charles Darwin born, 1809. A **Gaboon Viper** (*Bitis gabonica*) bit itself to death in the Philadelphia Zoological Gardens, 1963.

21

Last **Carolina Parakeet** (*Conuropsis carolinensis*) died in captivity, 1918.

26

Highest price paid for single pelts, mink-sable, US$2,700 per pelt, New York City, 1969.

28

Largest recorded **Elephant Seal** (*Mirounga angustirostris*) (22.5 feet /6.8 m, 12,200 lbs./5,534 kg) killed near Possession Bay, South Georgia, Antarctic Is., 1913.

11

THE TIGER OF THE AIR

The Great Horned Owl (*Bubo virginianus*) is a large and powerful bird ranging in length between 18 and 25 inches (46 and 64 cm), the female being much larger. It is probably the fiercest and most savage of our predatory birds, and has earned for itself the name "Tiger of the Air".

This species is usually fairly common in woodland tracts throughout North America from the timberline in the far north down into South America. Mainly non-migratory, it will shift its distribution to find better hunting when there is a scarcity of food.

The bulk of its prey consists of rabbits, rats, and mice, though it is classified as a general feeder. It will include in its diet a wide range of animals such as squirrels, woodchucks, cats, shrews, bats, grasshoppers, beetles, and birds ranging in size from sparrows to geese. The Great Horned Owl also preys upon snakes, fish, and scorpions. Attacks on such adversaries as skunks and porcupines are not uncommon; encounters with the latter often have fatal results for one or both contestants. It does, however, appear to have some immunity against the defensive weapon of the skunk, dreaded by many other creatures. When food is especially scarce it will attack poultry and game-birds, a practice frowned upon by poultrymen, farmers, and gamekeepers.

The Great Horned Owl has the distinction of being our earliest nester, and in parts of southern Canada will often nest as early as late February. The extremely early mating habits may be largely due to the long dependence that the young birds have on their parents. From the time the eggs hatch it generally takes ten weeks or so before the youngster is able to fly away and fend for itself. Consequently, the maturity of the Great Horned Owl coincides with that of birds that breed later and reach adulthood more quickly.

Although the marauding traits of these birds tend to make them most unpopular in some quarters, their usefulness as vermin exterminators cannot be overestimated. Owls are a very necessary part of any healthy wildlife community; their importance as natural predators cannot be too strongly emphasized.

GROUP OF BLUE JAYS

🌿 THE CAMP ROBBER 🌿

One of the most characteristic birds of the Canadian north woods is the Grey Jay (*Perisoreus canadensis*), one of the few northern resident birds which remains with us throughout the year.

The Grey Jay is known by a good many popular names, including Canada Jay, Whiskey John, Whiskey Jack, Carrion Bird, Meat Hawk, and Camp Robber. The last-mentioned name was bestowed upon the bird because of its habit of visiting camps of trappers and lumberjacks to steal anything remotely edible. It regards man as a benevolent provider of food and can become quite tame in his presence.

About twelve inches in length (30 cm), the Grey Jay bears a strong resemblance to an overgrown chickadee. Its feathers are a soft grey colour. Its neck is sooty black, and the forepart of its head is white. The wings and tail are of a darker shade of grey than the body. The Grey Jay possesses a wide variety of strange notes and calls, but most frequently utters a soft *whee-ah*. It is something of a mimic and any strange unidentifiable sound can generally be attributed to this bird.

It is one of our earliest nesting birds. Mating occurs in late winter, usually around February when the snow is still thick on the ground. The nest is bulky and substantial. One parent bird always remains with the greenish-grey, heavily spotted eggs until they hatch. It is remarkable the way the birds prevent the eggs from freezing in temperatures that may reach 30°F below zero (−34°C).

These curious birds tend to follow birders throughout their wanderings, repeatedly perching just above their heads and coming readily to the hand for food. They will often fly away with morsels of food in their bills only to return seconds later for further handouts. When hunger strikes, the Grey Jay will not disdain carrion. Its diet also includes a large number of injurious insects. ⌐∾

13

❧ CHISEL BILLS ❧

Woodpeckers have claws adapted to climbing and, in some instances, tails ending in stiff feathers with which they prop themselves upright while working on tree trunks. These wood-boring birds have bills as sharp and effective as chisels, enabling them to dig deep into trees to reach wood-destroying insects. These they extract with a long, barbed tongue that serves as a sort of fork; it is longer than the mouth of the bird and so is curled up when not in use. The Northern Three-toed Woodpecker (*Picoides tridactylus*) is particularly skilful and is a respected ally of the forester. Implacable foes of the bark beetle, these birds pursue their war against the enemies of the forest the year round.

The bill of the sapsucker is shorter than that of the woodpecker and thus its penetration is not as deep. The sapsucker's tongue ends in a brush-like form which it uses as a spoon. These birds can kill young trees by injuring the cambium — the source of the growth cells — but for this they compensate by consuming spiders, caterpillars, moths, and insect eggs and larvae. The Downy Woodpecker (*Picoides pubescens*) has a shorter bill; it cannot probe much deeper than the thickness of the bark from which it takes many crawling things. The Common Flicker (*Colaptes auratus*) spends less time on trees than on the ground where it digs immense quantities of ants and beetles. ∾

COMMON FLICKER

❝Canada Geese conduct themselves with dignity, never fight unless it's absolutely necessary to protect their families — and then their wrath is terrible. The gander takes only one mate in a lifetime, and I've never known one to make application for divorce.❞

Jack Miner

NORTHERN THREE-TOED WOODPECKER

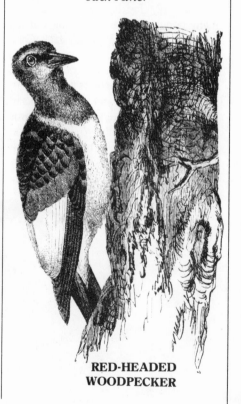

RED-HEADED WOODPECKER

FLITTER MOUSE

A bat's natural radar equipment enables it to avoid collision with obstacles by detecting the echo of its squeaks and chirps. The voices of some bats are pitched so extraordinarily high that the sounds are beyond the range of human hearing and can only be detected on the sensitive filament of a sound track.

Bats rival birds in their powers of flight and are among the most bizarre and unusual of nature's adaptations. The skin uniting their lengthened front and hind limbs and finger bones forms broad wings and helps to give them an extraordinary degree of manoeuvrability.

One of the most unusual character-istics of Big Brown Bats (*Eptesicus fuscus*) is that they bear from one to four young of which no more than two survive. When the young are very small, the mother bat flies from place to place with them clinging to her body. This practice is continued until the combined weight of the young exceeds her own.

In spite of their small size, bats are ferocious fighters; they will bare their teeth and fight viciously with little provocation. They will not, however, entangle themselves in your hair. ∾

THE SEA WOLF

Fearful of neither man nor beast, the Killer Whale (*Orcinus orca*) is renowned for its strength and ferocity. Although rarely exceeding 25 feet (8 m) in length, these large porpoises habitually attack whales several times their own size, often tearing the larger mammals to pieces.

One of the chief victims of "Orca" is the Californian Grey Whale (*Eschrichtius robustus*) which, although it attains a length of about 50 feet (15 m), becomes paralysed with fear when confronted by a pack of Killer Whales. At such times the Grey Whales will turn on their backs, with flippers outstretched, as they lie helpless at the surface.

Approaching its victim at high speed, a Killer Whale will put its nose against its victim's lips, force the mouth open, and gorge out great chunks of the soft, sponge-like tongue. At the same time, other Killer Whales are tearing at the giant body and literally eating the victim whale alive.

In captivity, the Killer Whale often displays great intelligence and strong affection for humans. ∾

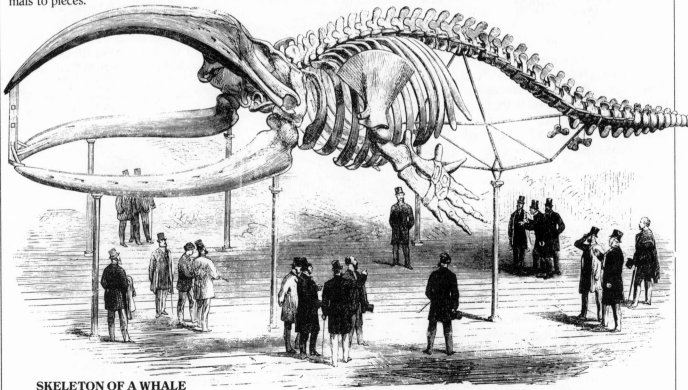

SKELETON OF A WHALE

NOT AS BLACK AS THEY'RE PAINTED

Farmers who try to keep Crows (*Corvus brachyrhynchos*) away from their corn by putting "scarecrows" in their fields find the birds virtually laughing at their feeble attempts to frighten them off. Crows are exceedingly wary and they seem to be able to judge accurately the range of a rifle. It is this cautiousness which enables them to survive against overwhelming odds. Two or three Crows will act as sentries for large flocks, perch-

ing on fence posts or in tall trees. A warning cry from one of them will send the entire flock winging away to safety.

Crows have acquired the unfortunate reputation of being blackguards and thieves; they have, indeed, been known to pull up sprouting corn, destroy chickens, and rob the nests of small birds. To their credit, however, they also consume large numbers of noxious insects, such as predacious beetles, and thereby do a considerable amount of good. ∾

OUR MOST PRIMITIVE BIRD

Of all our native birds, ornithologists place loons first on the scale of evolution since their bones show striking similarities to the fossilized remains of prehistoric birds. The loon is, therefore, our most primitive bird.

This characteristic bird of our north woods is best heard about the time you turn in for the night, although its far-echoing call also belongs to early morning and midday. Although it would seem that the loon never sleeps, it does so on the water. The bird's ability to dive is equalled by few other birds and it can overtake sizable fish.

Although widely distributed across most of Canada, the Common Loon (*Gavia immer*) is presently restricted almost entirely to the more remote waters where human populations are sparse. Usually there is only one pair to a lake, although large lakes may be found to contain more.

This large, handsome bird has been greatly persecuted in the past by the man with the gun, and has consequently disappeared from many of its former haunts. In more recent times it has been losing out on more remote waterways to summer cottagers and the outboard motor. Wise laws now protect this picturesque bird during all seasons, but it may be too late to restore the Common Loon to many of its former lakes. ∾

The Dipper (*Cinclus mexicanus*) or Water Ouzel has the cleanest house in town. The bird, about the size of a Sparrow, builds its nest under or behind a waterfall. Using its wings as flippers, it feeds on water insects and small fish while strolling fully submerged and unconcerned on the bottom of streams.

COMMON LOON

THE HARBINGER OF SPRING

HORNED LARK

The Horned Lark (*Eremophila alpestris*) is the very first of our migratory birds to arrive in the spring. The earliest authenticated date for such an arrival in Canada, according to the records of the late James L. Baillie, is February 3rd in the Toronto area. The reason they show up earlier than the other smaller birds is that they don't winter very far south.

While the snow is on the ground, they may be found in larger numbers in open fields wherever weed stalks are growing. They also tend to congregate along roadsides and highways so that they are easily seen from a car.

A small, buff-brown bird, little larger than a sparrow, the Horned Lark is distinctive by virtue of the black stripes on its forehead extending into black ear-tufts resembling horns: hence the bird's name. There is also a black patch on the breast and cheeks, while the face and throat are yellow.

RED-WINGED BLACKBIRD

Horned Larks are widely distributed, being found also in Europe and parts of Asia. In Britain, where it is known as the Shore Lark, it is uncommon, occurring on the east coast only as an occasional bird of passage.

Other early spring arrivals that may be

SONG SPARROWS

expected throughout the month of March are the Song Sparrow (*Melospiza melodia*), Red-winged Blackbird (*Agelaius phoeniceus*), Common Grackle (*Quiscalus quiscula*), Killdeer (*Charadrius vociferus*), Eastern Meadowlark (*Sturnella magna*), Ringed-necked Duck (*Aythya collaris*), and Cooper's Hawk (*Accipiter cooperii*).

For the most part these migratory birds adhere strictly to a rigid timetable, arriving at the same time each year, varying maybe a day or two from their schedule according to slight variations in climatic conditions. As weeks progress, many more species follow closely behind. Some species stay for a short time before continuing their journey farther north to their breeding grounds. Others remain throughout the summer months to enhance the countryside with their beauty and song. ∾

MEADOWLARK

17

WAPITI CHASED BY WOLVES

The Cougar (*Felis concolor*) is known by many names, including Puma (in South America), Mountain Lion, Panther, Painter, Catamount, Screamer, Indian Devil, and King Cat. This large cat was a feared enemy of the earliest North American settlers because it frequently raided their livestock and occasionally attacked the settlers themselves. Generally speaking, however, although the cougar is powerful enough to kill a man, it is a solitary and shy animal and it prefers to shun humans.

The cougar has long been banished from most of Canada. It once had the greatest range of any New World mammal and was found from northern British Columbia east to Nova Scotia and south to Patagonia at the tip of South America. Now, it is confined to the forested regions of British Columbia and Alberta.

KING CAT

Man and the cougar could not live on the same ground. The cougars retreated, gradually vanishing with the wilderness. Previously subjected, like most large predators, to the ravages of the bounty system, cougars today are generally regarded as game animals.

Although deer constitutes the mainstay of its diet, the cougar will also take beavers, rabbits, and birds, down to prey as small as mice and frogs. Although field studies show that cougars do take healthy deer as well as the weak, sick, and disabled, it is generally conceded that their presence keeps the deer alert and vigorous, helping to prevent overpopulation and resulting malnutrition. Those rare individuals that do attack man and cattle are hunted down by professional hunters in the employ of provincial agencies. ∾

CALENDAR

1

Yellowstone National Park founded (1st national park in U.S.), 1872.

2

Earliest recorded date for a **Cuckoo** in Britain (Wantage, Oxford), 1972.

3

Convention on International Trade in Endangered Fauna signed in Washington D.C., 1973.

7

A cat fell 120 feet (36 m) from its owner's flat in Maida Vale, London, England, and landed unhurt, 1965.

11

Last **Heath Hen** (*Tympanuchus cupido cupido*) died on Martha's Vineyard, Massachusetts, 1932.

20

Turkey Vultures (*Cathartes aura*) return to Hinckly, Ohio (Buzzard Day).

24

Longest-lived Deer, a **Red Deer** (*Cervus elaphus*), died, at age 26.5 years, in the National Zoological Park, Washington D.C., 1941.

26

La Salle landed at Point Pelee, Ontario, during his expedition to the Ohio Valley, 1669.

COUGARS

COMMON GANNET

THE GANNETS OF BONAVENTURE ISLAND

Just two miles (3 km) from the Quebec village of Percé, in the Gulf of St. Lawrence, lies Bonaventure Island. Here are to be found some of the most spectacular sea-bird colonies to be seen anywhere. In particular, Bonaventure is world-renowned for its colony of Gannets (*Morus bassanus*), and upwards of 18,000 pairs of these birds inhabit this island, making this colony the largest of the twenty-two gannetries known throughout the world.

The adult gannet is a magnificent, large white bird growing up to forty inches (102 cm) in length with a wing span of up to six feet (183 cm). Its body is distinctly streamlined by being tapered at both ends. The wing tips are jet black and the head and neck are saffron yellow. In the first year, the young bird is dark slatey-brown, spotted with white. As the young bird matures, the brown feathers are replaced by the splendid, white adult plumage. Gannets feed on fish and obtain their food by making spectacular plunges head first into the ocean from a distance of a hundred feet (3,048 cm) or so.

Bonaventure Island, discovered by Jacques Cartier during his first exploration of the New World in 1534, has suffered for 400 years from human settlement and exploitation. By the beginning of this century, some of the bird colonies were showing definite signs of decline. At that time, the gannet colony had been depleted to about 3,000 birds, but with the Migratory Bird Convention Act (1917), the island became a sanctuary. On March 29, 1919, the eastern and northern cliffs of Bonaventure Island, together with Percé Rock, were declared federal migratory bird sanctuaries under the control of the Canadian Wildlife Service. Under protection, the gannet popu-

lations have steadily increased and are now estimated to be at 36,000 to 50,000 strong, enough to whiten the cliff top and spill over onto the slopes. Other coastal breeding birds include: the Common Murre (*Uria aalge*), Razorbill (*Alca torda*), Black Guillemot (*Cepphus*

BLACK GUILLEMOT

grylle), Black-legged Kittiwake (*Rissa tridactyla*), Common Puffin (*Fratercula arctica*), Herring Gull (*Larus argentatus*), Double-crested Cormorant (*Phalacrocorax auritus*), Great Black-backed Gull (*Larus marinus*), and Leach's Storm Petrel (*Oceanodroma leucorhoa*).

KITTIWAKE

COMMON GANNET

The dean of American ornithologists, Roger Tory Peterson, is obviously much impressed with Bonaventure Island. He expresses his enthusiasm in glowing terms:

"I believe the gannet ledges of Bonaventure to be one of the greatest ornithological spectacles on the continent, more impressive even than the populous murre and auk colonies further north. The size and whiteness of the gannets give them a visual impact lacking in lesser fowl."

Bonaventure Island is reached by boat from the village of Percé. Regular boat tours run by private operators circle the island and enable passengers to observe the sea-bird colonies from the water. Visitors are also able to ramble along the many trails. A guided tour of the island is also conducted by the staff of the Percé Wildlife Centre to help the visitor explore the varied habitats filled with fascinating stories.

For further information on Bonaventure Island write to:

Centre d'Histoire Naturelle de Percé,
Percé Comté,
Gaspé, Québec
G0C 2L0 ∾

ATLANTIC PUFFIN

THE ANIMAL THAT FOUNDED A FUR INDUSTRY

No other animal has influenced a nation to the extent that the American Beaver (*Castor canadensis*) has influenced the development of Canada. The beaver was exploited from the outset for its rich, dense fur, and began to decline in numbers as early as 1638, when the compulsory use of fur in the manufacture of hats was decreed by King Charles I.

Fashionable Europeans demanded felt hats, and the soft beaver fur made the most luxurious felt of all. Hat styles varied considerably in size and shape; some hats were tall, some squat, and others drooping. The beaver-hat industry became increasingly important and the pelts themselves became the major fur export of Canada. This predominance lasted for two hundred years and makes the beaver the best example of a fur-bearing animal whose numbers were drastically affected by the exploitation of man. The history of the fur trade is essentially a history of the beaver.

Beaver fur was popular in part because the animal was so widespread and numerous. And this popularity endured for several decades as fur trappers spread out across the continent seeking new colonies of beavers as earlier stocks diminished. Up to 17,000 beaver pelts a year were taken to be sold in London and Edinburgh, most being used for felt to make beaver hats. Indians were encouraged to kill far more beavers than they required and to trade their surplus skins to the white man. One beaver pelt would buy a pound (0.45 kg) of tobacco; twelve would buy a gun. The high regard in which the beaver was held by the Indians in no way impeded its destruction; the progress of civilization was everywhere accompanied by its extirpation.

With the founding of the Hudson's Bay Company in 1670, the fur trade became the chief business of the colonies, exceeding in importance the earlier commerce in timber and fish. With the use of steel traps, trapping became more and more effective. By 1812 beavers were scarce everywhere in Canada east of the Rocky Mountains. They were still plentiful in the west, but trapping

21

BEAVER

would later reduce their numbers there also, and shortly after the turn of the century beavers become scarce in western Canada.

The beaver had become extirpated throughout much of the continent and, in fact, had the French and Italian stylists not shifted their interest to the silk hat, the beaver might have followed the Great Auk and Passenger Pigeon to extinction.

In the early 1930s, beaver fur management was developed among the Indian trappers of northern Ontario. This practice was highly successful and quickly spread right across Canada, with the result that the beaver populations dramatically increased. Unfortunately, with the resurgence of the beaver population, the problem of nuisance beavers has appeared. The dams plug culverts, thereby flooding roads, bridges, railway lines, and agricultural lands, and beavers cut down ornamental trees on the edges of towns, cities, golf courses, and parks. As a result, provincial game departments have been forced to maintain regular programs of live trapping and moving the offending beavers to unstocked areas.

Despite their destructiveness, beavers are natural conservationists. The multi-

tudes of beavers on the headwaters of major streams stabilize stream flow and prevent erosion. Also, they create trout ponds, and improve the habitat for many forms of wildlife such as ducks and Woodcocks (*Scolopax minor*), the Great Blue Heron (*Ardea herodius*), and mammals such as Mink (*Mustela vison*) and Otter (*Lutra canadensis*). Therefore, they merit careful study and intelligent management. Deprived of the activities of the beaver, forest streams would lose much of their variety and life.

66 'Tis a great pity,...that none of these wonderful Creatures were found in the *Tyber*, or in the Territories of *Parnassus*; what fine Things would the *Greek* and *Roman* Poets have said on this Subject! 99

Pierre-Francois-Xavier de Charlevoix, "On Beavers" (1720)

MINK

THE ROBIN

Of all Canadian birds, there is none that comes into more intimate contact with man than does the American Robin (*Turdus migratorius*).

The early English colonists gave it its name, doubtless because it resembled in colouration the Robin Redbreast (*Enthacus rubecula*) of England, but they failed to notice the close relationship between the American Robin and the European Blackbird (*Turdus merula*). The two birds, both thrushes, are very similar in habit, general deportment, and voice, although different in plumage. They are, in fact, equivalent species ecologically. The spotted breasts of these birds is indicative of their affiliation to the thrushes, a fact that all members of the genus *"Turdus"* show in the younger stages.

Before the forests were cleared, robins built mainly on horizontal limbs of trees or in crotches between the branches as many robins build now in the wilder, more heavily wooded parts of the country. But when man felled the trees and replaced them with buildings, the bird was supplied with countless additional sites which afforded ample support, the chief requirement for a robin to build a nest.

Although the robin is an efficient aid to the agriculturalist, its fondness for fruit occasionally gets it into trouble with raisers of small fruit, especially cherries. Forty-two per cent of its food is animal, mostly insects; the remainder is composed largely of berries and other soft, small fruits, of which little more than one per cent is cultivated fruit. ๛

THE MALIGNED GRIZZLY

Although they have the potential to be dangerous, Grizzly Bears (*Ursus arctos horribilis*) are generally shy creatures of nocturnal habit and the appearance of a human usually puts them to flight. Unprovoked attacks by Grizzlies are very rare; they are most often preceded by one of three acts: approaching a female with young at close range, approaching a bear in possession of a carcass, or surprising a bear at close range.

The early settlers saw the Grizzly as a powerful beast with catholic eating habits. They felt threatened by this large animal and the results were predictable: the Grizzly is now extinct in almost all the eastern parts of its range.

The Grizzly was the first predator to be persecuted by cattle ranchers. Bounties for dead bears were offered by the Cattleman's and Sheep Grower's Association and by local and provincial governments. Modern firearms and trained dogs were used to drive the Grizzly from its native haunts. Not even the rattlesnake has had such a determined and widespread campaign of elimination waged against it.

Poison became a common method of destroying the Grizzly. Carcases of sheep, cattle, deer, elk, and moose which men thought would attract the Grizzly were poisoned with strychnine and large numbers of the animal were wiped out. Many other species were also killed by

the poison. Prior to the use of poison, steel bear traps were used by trappers and a crueller device has yet to be invented.

In order to escape, the animal has been known to chew through its bones and limp off, leaving its foot in the trap. ๛

One of the most outstanding of Canada's early naturalists and wildlife painters was a little-known immigrant from England named William Pope.

William Pope was born in 1811 in Maidstone, Kent, England, and from the time he was a small boy would roam the local countryside as he developed an interest in the outdoors and the natural world around him. As a young man, he had heard great tales of the abundant wildlife and excellent hunting that was to be had in Canada, and on Good Friday, March 28, 1834, he set sail on the steamship *Ontario*, arriving at New York some six weeks later.

William Pope settled in the Long Point area of southwestern Ontario, and almost immediately proceeded to paint and sketch the fauna and flora of that region. By 1837 he had completed more than forty bird paintings which included the Whip-Poor-Will, Passenger Pigeon, Yellow-bellied Sapsucker, Spotted Sandpiper, Mourning Dove, and other spring species. In his daily journals Pope mentioned certain birds he found to be common that are no longer in evidence, such as the Passenger Pigeon, Wild Turkey, and Red-bellied Woodpecker, together with large numbers of different species of hawks and owls.

During the months of June and July, Pope settled into a routine of hunting and collecting birds in the morning, and devoting his afternoons to painting. He was interested in everything around him; nothing escaped his keen eye or ear. However, roughing it in the backwoods, the terrible food, the humidity, and especially the mosquitoes made him long for the comforts of civilization, and he headed for a six-week tour of the United States, eventually returning to England. Here he was to remain for the next seven years.

William Pope returned to Canada with a bride, Martha Mills, and settled in the Port Rowan area. In 1846 the Popes returned to England to collect an inheritance, and remained there for five years before returning to Upper Canada where they took up residence at Chestnut Grove, near Vittoria. A second inheritance in 1854 precipitated another and final trip to England.

When William Pope died in 1902, he left behind a legacy of over 200 watercolours, together with journals and diaries which are historically valuable for their insights into life in Upper Canada. In 1916, John Ross Robertson, founder of *The Toronto Telegram*, acquired 226 of these pictures and donated them to the Toronto Public Library.

The Pope paintings, particularly those dated in the 1830s and 1840s, are certainly some of the best examples of early wildlife art in Canada. Undoubtedly, had his work been made public during his lifetime, he would have received substantial recognition. However, William Pope appears to have been financially independent and not one to entertain commercial aspirations with respect to his paintings. Rather, he was a man who loved the outdoors, especially hunting and gathering birds, and he kept meticulous notes in his journals which now tell a story of the natural history of Upper Canada at that time.

The journals are in the possession of the Lawson Memorial Library at the University of Western Ontario, and the paintings have resided since 1917 in the Baldwin Room of the Central Library in Toronto. ᴄᴧ

AMERICAN BARN OWL

HOUSE SPARROWS

APRIL

Certain members of the butterfly family *"Nymphalidae"* hibernate throughout the entire winter in the adult butterfly stage, concealing themselves in hollows in tree trunks, under large stones or logs, in the corners of barns and outhouses, and in other suitable refuges.

They are always the first butterflies to appear as soon as the weather is warm and sunny enough for their liking. Very often, an unusually warm day in mid-winter will temporarily bring them forth from their hiding places, and one may see the incongruous sight of butterflies flying against a background of snow.

By far the most common of this group of butterflies is the Mourning Cloak (*Nymphalis antiopa*), which is fairly widespread throughout most of the

WEST VIRGINIA WHITE BUTTERFLY

Danyl Stewt.

FIRST BUTTERFLY OF SPRING

North American continent in wooded areas and open country. Somewhat slug-

gish after their long winter sleep they flitter about awhile only to rest with wings extended on the ground, often remaining motionless for some time.

A freshly emerged adult Mourning Cloak is a strikingly beautiful insect, although most early-spring specimens tend to get rather ragged and worn throughout their hibernation period. The butterfly is a rich maroon-brown with a light yellow border along the outer margins of its wings. There are a number of irregularly shaped large blue spots inset in black running along the inside of the pale-coloured border. In England, where it occurs only as a vary rare migrant from Scandinavia, this butterfly is known by the delightful name of "Camberwell Beauty" and is greatly prized by collectors.

1

Migrating **Whistling Swans** (*Cygnus columbianus*) stop over at Long Point, Ontario.

13

Archibald Belaney (Grey Owl) died, 1938.

CALENDAR

15

Mourning Cloak (*Nymphalis antiopa*) butterflies emerge from hibernation.

17

John Macoun, Canadian naturalist, born, 1832.

18

First **Whooping Crane** (*Grus americana*) egg laid in captivity, 1975.

19

Record European lobster caught near Corsica, France (35¼ lbs./16 kg), 1966.

20

Eurasian Golden Plover (*Charadrius apricarius*) in Canada (Avalon Peninsula, Newfoundland), 1961.

23

Beaver (*Castor canadensis*) on first Canadian postage stamp, 1851.

BUTTERFLIES

QUESTION MARK

MILBERT'S TORTOISE SHELL

Although Canada does not compare with the tropics for its variety of butterflies, we do have a number of attractive species that are worthy of more than passing interest. It is encouraging to note that some of the more splendid species, such as the Canadian Tiger (*Papilio glaucus canadensis*) and Eastern Black Swallowtail (*P. polyxenes asterias*), the Monarch (*Danaus plexippus*) and Mourning Cloak (*Nymphalis antiopa*), are all fairly common over much of Canada.

In the distribution of butterflies in Canada, there is a faunal change on either side of the Rocky Mountains, some species on one side not being found at all on the other. In some cases, however, there are very closely related species that may appear to be identical.

All butterflies in Canada, except the Monarch, hibernate throughout the winter in their various stages, the majority as pupae, but many also hibernate in the egg, larval (caterpillar), and adult stages. Those that hibernate as adults are the first to appear in the spring. An exceptionally warm period in late winter will often bring them forth and sometimes you will see butterflies flying about while the snow is still thick on the ground.

The life span of a butterfly is generally two to three weeks although the hibernators and migrating Monarchs may live for almost ten months. A female butterfly may lay from 200 to 500 eggs, but only a minute proportion will ever reach majority. Butterflies, in both larval and adult form, have many predators that take an enormous toll on their population, the most common being birds, lizards, beetles, mice, and spiders. The greatest peril of all is the parasitic wasps and flies that deposit their eggs in the eggs or larvae of butterflies. The emerging parasite eats away at the inside of its host, eventually devouring it.

It would appear that longevity in butterflies is inversely correlated to the amount of energy expended by them. Experiments have shown that when certain caterpillars were decapitated in such a way as to cause the minimum blood-loss, they could continue the natural course of their development and, after passing through the chrysalis stage, emerge as perfectly healthy but headless

BANDED PURPLE

butterflies. Scientists who have studied this phenomenon have come to the conclusion that headless butterflies are longer lived because they lead a much less active life. A perfect butterfly quickly spends its strength in activity, whereas its headless companions, leading more placid lives, wear out their vital forces at a slower rate and attain a comparatively extended lifespan. ∾

MONARCH BUTTERFLY

PAINTED LADY BUTTERFLY

The Hognose Snake stakes its life on its acting ability. When threatened, it inflates and widens its head in a gesture to scare off an enemy. If this tactic fails, the snake goes on to Act II: it falls into a fit of convulsions, writhing in agony, its mouth gaping around a lolling tongue. Finally, it rolls on its back in a grotesque death scene. A bad performance can be terminal.

MONARCH OF THE NORTH WOODS

Moose (*Alces alces*) have few natural enemies, but are preyed upon by wolves to some extent. Wolves have difficulty killing moose, however, for they are formidable fighters, using their large hoofs as weapons. As a game animal they are eagerly hunted by man, both for their large quantity of meat and for their tremendous palmated antlers which may measure six feet (183 cm) from tip to tip. The antlers are shed annually and the new ones are at first covered by "velvet" such as seen on the more familiar White-tailed Deer (*Odocoileus virginianus*).

There is no more thrilling sight than

that of a fully antlered moose, but if we are going to share their country we must learn to live with them. Although less common than deer, in several ways moose present a greater driving hazard, because they move more slowly and are more likely to be standing in the middle of the road or wandering the highway on a dark night. In this way, many of these huge animals are killed each year. Moderate speeds and watchful driving are necessary to avoid this terrible carnage.

PRICKLY RODENT

The American Porcupine (*Erethizon dorsatum*) is a strong and heavy animal that may weigh up to thirty pounds (14 kg); except for the damage it does by chewing any article that may contain a trace of salt, it is quite harmless as long as you keep your distance.

It may seem like a strange comparison, but the porcupine and the elephant have this much in common: they both have a very low reproductive rate and yet continue to thrive in the face of much opposition, and increase rapidly under undisturbed conditions. The porcupine does not breed until it is three years old, and then produces only one young at a time (rarely two). The young are very well developed at birth and are able to use their quills for protection within a few hours. They become independent of their mothers within a few months.

There is only one species of porcupine in North America, but similar animals are found almost throughout the world; there is a variety of these creatures in Central and South America. Despite their quills, porcupines are preyed upon by Fishers (*Martes pennanti*), wolves, and foxes. Contrary to popular opinion, they are not able to shoot their quills.

NORWAY RAT

IMMIGRANT RODENTS

The Brown or Norway Rat (*Rattus norvegicus*) and the House Mouse (*Mus musculus*) are immigrants to this continent. Both species have adapted especially well to man-made habitats and may be found close to human habitation.

The Norway Rat is believed to have been native to the more temperate climate of Asia. It appeared in Europe and the British Isles during the eighteenth century; in 1727, the species swept westward across the Volga River. Boarding ships bound for America from numerous European and British ports, the Norway Rat reached the Upper St.

Lawrence region about 1775 and Ottawa about 1890. Once established, local populations of the Norway Rat exploded with remarkable rapidity.

The House Mouse originally hailed from southwestern Persia (now Iran) and probably stowed away on the first caravans and ships which carried goods on land and water routes to most parts of the world. Weighing only half an ounce (14 g), it is no wonder that this tiny rodent travelled undetected in shipments of clothing, food, and household effects until the items were unpacked and its ravages discovered. ∽

COMMON MOUSE

PROTECTIVE COLOURATION

Most lower forms of animal life depend upon a resemblance to their surroundings to render them inconspicuous. In this way they acquire both protection from predators and an advantage over their own prey.

The American Woodcock (*Scolopax minor*) is an excellent example of the use of protective colouration, as every sportsman will concur. This popular game bird is a denizen of alder swamps and moist beech groves where its rusty-

RUFFED GROUSE

coloured plumage perfectly matches the brown leaves and grass: it is virtually invisible to even the keenest eye. Since the woodcock drives its three-inch (8 cm) bill deep into the ground in its search for worms, it never sees what it eats. During the course of evolution, the bird's eyes have migrated up and back towards the top of its head so that when it is engaged in feeding it can watch for its enemies from a range of vision greater than the norm for most species.

The Ruffed Grouse (*Bonasa umbellus*) is equally well protected, as are the Nighthawk (*Chordeiles minor*) and the Whip-Poor-Will (*Caprimulgus vociferus*) which reinforce their protective resemblance by habitually resting lengthwise on a limb. It is only by sheer chance that a nighthawk can be distinguished from a piece of bark. ∽

RING-NECKED PHEASANTS

WOODCOCK

THE RAFT BUILDER

The Pied-billed Grebe (*Podilymbus podiceps*), whose range is throughout most of North America, is known popularly as "the water witch". It can dive at the flash of a gun and be under the surface of the water before the shot reaches it. The grebe sinks down into the water with only the bill and eyes showing above the surface and remains there until the danger has passed.

The most remarkable thing about this bird, however, is its choice of a home.

HORNED GREBE

Unlike most water birds that build their nests in sand or on rocks, the grebe builds its nest on the water. From the buoyant stems of water plants, the female bird makes a small, floating platform with a slight depression in the centre for her eggs. The raft is attached to the reeds so that it can float from side to side but will not drift away. The eggs are covered up and then disguised as a mass of floating vegetation. ∽

THE WHISTLER

The Hoary Marmot (*Marmota caligata*), a western counterpart of the familiar Groundhog (*Marmota monax*), inhabits the upper slopes of the western Rocky Mountains, where it is commonly preyed upon by the Golden Eagle (*Aquila chrysaetos*) and the Grizzly Bear (*Ursus arctos horribilis*).

Large raptors and carnivores are a constant threat to the marmots whenever these gregarious rodents go into the open to feed. However, to guard themselves against these maraudings they have devised an air-raid protection system. Whenever one of the marmots observes a predator it emits a piercing whistle which, in effect, acts as an air-raid warning to others. The rodents then take shelter in their shallow burrows where they are well protected.

There can be little doubt that the whistle of the Hoary Marmot is the shrillest, farthest-reaching sound issued by a mammal; the sound can be heard at a distance of a mile (1.6 km) and, under the most favourable conditions, at twice that distance.

Once the marmot has given the alarm, it also goes underground. When the danger has passed it utters another, somewhat lower-pitched, whistle, in effect the "all clear". Then grey heads pop up all over the mountainside and normal marmot activities resume once again. ∽

The largest and most fearsome of the invertebrates is the Giant Squid (*Architeuthis longimanus*) found on the Newfoundland Banks. Its body is more than 8 feet (244 cm) long and the two longest of its ten snake-like arms may measure up to 35 feet (11 m). With this powerful set of weapons, it gives a good fight to its worst natural enemy, the Sperm Whale.

GROUNDHOG

CAPTIVE-BRED PEREGRINES

In order to prevent the Peregrine Falcon (*Falco peregrinus*) from becoming extinct in Canada, the Canadian Wildlife Service began a captive-rearing program in 1970. In that year, twelve immature birds were taken into captivity at the service's facility at Wainwright, near Edmonton, to provide the nucleus for the breeding program.

The most successful technique used to date has been "fostering" or placing captive-bred eggs or young under wild parents of the species. Another technique used successfully is known as "double-clutching" and involves taking the first clutch of eggs and thereby forcing the pair to lay again. In 1974 clutches of eggs were taken from two wild pairs of Peregrine Falcons and three of five fertile eggs were hatched. The young were then raised in captivity until they were about three weeks old and were then given back to the original parents.

In the interim the birds had laid and hatched another three or four fertile eggs. The newly hatched young were then all placed in one of the nests while their

older (by three weeks) siblings were placed in the second nest. All of these young birds were then fledged successfully by the adults.

Peregrine Falcons from these captive-breeding programs have been subsequently reintroduced into the wild with most encouraging results. ∽

THE SMALLEST ANIMALS

Canada has the distinction of playing host to some of the smallest wildlife species in the world.

The smallest native bird, the Calliope Hummingbird (*Stellula calliope*), is also one of the world's smallest; the Least Weasel (*Mustela nivalis*) is the smallest of all carnivores; and the Pygmy Shrew (*Microsorex hoyi*) is the most diminutive mammal on the continent.

The Calliope Hummingbird, native to a small area of south-central British Columbia, weighs, on average, about one-tenth of an ounce (2.8 g). However, despite its size, it doesn't hesitate to attack much larger birds when necessary and even threatens large hawks.

The Least Weasel is believed to be the rarest mammal in eastern Canada, although it is considerably more common in the west. It is easily identified by its short tail which does not have a black tip but may have a few black hairs. Its skull is smaller and more smoothly

WEASELS

rounded than that of other weasels.

The Pygmy Shrew is found throughout eastern Canada with the exception of Newfoundland. This smallest North American mammal rarely weighs more than a dime when fully grown. Continuously active during its waking period, the

Pygmy Shrew progresses with sudden, rapid movements, at the same time uttering short, sharp squeaks. All this activity means that the animal requires continuous food to sustain it, together with plenty of sleep which the shrew has curled up in a ball. ∽

33

NARWHALS

Canada is generally considered to be a northern country and for the most part this is correct. Vast spruce-fir forests extend from coast to coast in a never-ending chain. In the extreme north are the tundra and high arctic, a wilderness of ice and snow, almost inaccessible and visited rarely by a few stout-hearted individuals.

There is, however, a small area of Canada with an environment similar to parts of the southern United States, with the same latitude as northern California and enjoying the same favourable, balmy weather.

When the first settlers arrived in Canada, they found a thickly wooded area of hardwood trees ranging in a continuous belt along the north shore of Lake Erie in southwestern Ontario, extending north to Sarnia and Toronto — the only true region of deciduous forest in Canada.

BOG TURTLE

CANADA'S DEEP SOUTH

Unfortunately, this unique area was chosen as the centre of urban and industrial development and most of the virgin forest soon came under the axe. Today,

there are only a few scattered areas where any sizable hardwood forests still remain in Canada. Point Pelee is such a place.

Geographically, Point Pelee is a spit of sand some nine miles (15 km) long, jutting into Lake Erie; the terrain is mostly marsh and woodland. The major part of the park is a 2,000-acre (809 ha) marsh comprising many large ponds. Many diversified forms of wildlife are found at Pelee. Undoubtedly, its greatest claim to fame is as one of the finest birdwatching spots on the continent during the annual spring migration. Certainly, the finest in Canada.

From March until June, warm air currents carry many rare birds northwards across Lake Erie to Pelee where they arrive exhausted and hungry. Birds of all species may be found in profusion, and rarities turn up so often that they are

---

2

Hudson's Bay Company granted charter, 1670. **Tufted Titmouse** (*Parus bicolor*) first reported in Canada (Point Pelee), 1914.

8

Little Egret (*Egretta garzetta*) reported for Canada (Conception Bay, Newfoundland), 1954. Longest-lived snake (31 years old), an **Anaconda,** died in Basle Zoological Gardens, Switzerland, 1962.

9

Percy Taverner, Canadian ornithologist, died, 1947.

10-12

Peak of spring migration at Point Pelee.

CALENDAR

13

Kirtland's Warbler (*Dendroica kirtlandii*) discovered near Cleveland, Ohio, 1851. **Yellow-green Vireo** (*Vireo flavoviridis*) reported for Canada (Godbout, Quebec), 1883.

16

Evening Bat (*Nycticeius humeralis*) reported for Canada (Point Pelee, Ontario), 1911.

18

Last recorded **Passenger Pigeon** (*Ectopistes migratorius*) in Canada (Penetanguishene, Ontario), 1902.

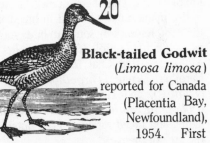

20

Black-tailed Godwit (*Limosa limosa*) reported for Canada (Placentia Bay, Newfoundland), 1954. First **Bewick's Wren** (*Thryomanes bewickii*) nest reported for Canada (Point Pelee, Ontario), 1950. First occurrence of **Mockingbird** (*Mimus polyglottos*) in Canada (Point Pelee, Ontario), 1906.

21

Chuck-will's-Widow (*Caprimulgus carolinensis*) seen in Canada (Point Pelee, Ontario), 1906.

24

Whimbrels (*Numenius phaeopus*) migrate through Toronto, Ontario.

YELLOW-BREASTED CHAT

almost taken for granted. The height of the spring migration occurs around mid-May when the warbler wave is under way. At this time, the park is literally alive with birds, and the early morning choruses have to be heard to be believed. On a good day it is not unusual to record over a hundred different species of birds.

Sometimes waves of birds will appear in astronomical numbers. As many as 20,000 White-throated Sparrows (*Zonotrichia albicollis*) have been recorded in a single day, as well as 6,000 Red-breasted Mergansers (*Mergus serrator*), 1,000 Barn Swallows (*Hirundo rustica*), and 650 Whistling Swans (*Cygnus columbianus*).

Though most birds seen at Pelee are migrants and end their journey farther north, many remain behind to breed in the park. Essentially southern birds such as the Orchard Oriole (*Icterus spurius*), Yellow-breasted Chat (*Icteria virens*), Carolina Wren (*Thryothorus ludovicianus*), and Blue-grey Gnatcatcher (*Polioptila caerulea*) are summer residents, and breed rarely, if ever, outside the area of the park.

The autumn migration is, in its way, no less interesting than that of the spring. During the latter part of September, large gatherings of hawks, in particular the Sharp-shinned Hawk (*Accipiter striatus*), put on a spectacular show prior to their long flight south.

Reptiles and amphibians are also very prominent at Pelee; in fact, there are probably more turtles found at Point Pelee than anywhere else in Canada. Characteristic species include the Five-lined Skink (*Eumeces fasciatus*), Eastern Spiny Softshell Turtle (*Trionyx spiniferus*), and Fowler's Toad (*Bufo woodhousei fowleri*), a smaller cousin of the more familiar American Toad (*Bufo*

americanus). The Five-lined Skink is eastern Canada's only lizard, and when young is endowed with a vivid blue tail, hence its other common name of "Blue-tailed Skink". Other rare and indigenous animals include the Blanchard's Cricket Frog (*Acris crepitans blanchardi*), Eastern Mole (*Scalopus aquaticus*), Eastern Fox Squirrel (*Sciurus niger*), Evening Bat (*Nycticeius humeralis*) (probably accidental), and Northern Katydid (*Pterophylla camellefolia*).

Point Pelee is, of course, a bonanza for botanists. The growth of shrubs in the park is luxuriant. Six hundred plant species are found here, mostly along the woodland nature trail. Wildflowers also

grow profusely. Among the most notable are Flowering Spurge, Wild Potato-vine, Swamp Mallow, and Prickly Pear Cactus (probably the only area in eastern Canada where it is found). Characteristically southern trees include Black Walnut, Red Mulberry, Cottonwood, Sycamore, White Sassafras, Chestnut Oak, and Red Cedar.

Butterflies and other insects abound at Point Pelee, and the Giant Swallowtail (*Papilio cresphontes*), the largest butterfly to be found in eastern North America, in some years is not uncommon in the park. It is boldly coloured with yellow blotches and spots on a brown background, and is another reminder of

METAMORPHOSES OF THE MOLE CRICKET

GIANT SWALLOWTAIL

the tropics where it originated. Similar species also identical in appearance are found commonly throughout tropical America. While on the subject of butterflies, one cannot ignore the familiar Monarch (*Danaus plexippus*). Sometimes huge congregations of migrating Monarchs festoon the shrubs and trees, resting prior to their long flight to central Mexico.

One particularly interesting insect found here is the Mole Cricket (*Gryllotalpa hexadactyla*), a small, dark brown insect about an inch (25 mm) in length which burrows and tunnels in the damp soil about the margins of streams and ponds, sometimes to a depth of about eight inches (20 cm). It is so called because its method of burrowing is similar to that of the mole with its short, broad front legs. It chirps in the same way as other crickets. Again, this is a southern species and found in Canada only around Point Pelee and the surrounding district.

It should be strongly emphasized that collecting plants or other specimens, or the molesting of animals in any way is strictly forbidden at Pelee. Park rangers are especially alert to any infringement and strongly enforce this ruling. Many an avid butterfly collector has been evicted from the park.

During the late spring and summer, an interpretative service is maintained and park naturalists are on hand to help with questions and provide organized and illustrated talks and field trips. The purpose of Point Pelee National Park is to preserve this unique part of Canada's wild environment and to educate visitors to a better understanding and appreciation of the local natural treasures.

Point Pelee National Park is located six miles south of Leamington, which can be reached from Highway 401. Further enquiries should be addressed to:
Superintendent,
Pointe Pelee National Park,
R.R. #1,
Leamington, Ontario
N8H 3V4 ∽

MIGRATION DATES

Migration patterns for birds have remained the same over the years with arrival and departure times varying by only a few days. The following are the migration dates for the species that pass through Point Pelee National Park, which is a focal point in migration. This spot lies along both the Mississippi and Atlantic flyways, and is frequented by species nesting from the Prairies to Quebec and the Arctic.

Spring	Start of Build up	Peak
Loons and Grebes	Apr. 1	Apr. 15
Swans, Geese and Ducks	Apr. 10	Apr. 20
Shorebirds	May 5	May 20
Gulls	Mar. 20	May 20
Terns	Apr. 15	May 1
Cuckoos		
Hummingbirds		
Flycatchers		
Swallows		
Jays		
Thrushes	May 5	May 15
Wrens		
Waxwings		
Vireos		
Warblers		
Finches		

Fall	Start of Build up	Peak
Ducks	Sept. 10	Sept. 30
Geese	Oct. 10	Oct. 20
Hawks	Oct. 25	Nov. 10
Shorebirds	Sept. 10	Sept. 20
Yellowlegs		
Pectoral Sandpiper	July 30	Aug. 5
Sanderling		
Plovers	Oct. 1	Oct. 10
Terns	Aug. 25	Sept. 10
Cuckoos		
Hummingbirds		
Flycatchers		
Wrens	Aug. 15	Sept. 5
Vireos		
Warblers		
Owls	Oct. 15	Oct. 25
Blackbirds	Oct. 15	Oct. 30
Sparrows	Oct. 15	Oct. 30
Thrushes	Sept. 15	Sept. 25

BIRDWATCHERS' EQUIPMENT

Birdwatching has become an increasingly popular pastime in North America in recent years. The number of birders, in fact, has quadrupled since the end of the Second World War. Its charm undoubtedly lies in the fact that all persons can participate, amateur and professional, old and young alike. Also, the necessary equipment is both simple and inexpensive. All that is required is a good, serviceable pair of binoculars and a pocket field guide.

HORNED LARK

The purchase of a pair of binoculars is largely a matter of personal choice. Most birders prefer binoculars with a magnification between 7 x 35 and 8 x 50. There are a number of good foreign-made models at present that can be purchased at a reasonable cost. The rule of thumb with binoculars should be to purchase the best that your pocket will allow.

WHIP-POOR-WILL

As for field guides, the most popular and widely used in Canada would appear to be *Birds of North America* by Chandler S. Robbins, Bertel Bruun, Herbert S. Zim, and Arthur Singer, and *A Field Guide to the Birds of Western North America* and *A Field Guide to the Birds of Eastern North America* by Roger Tory Peterson. The last mentioned book has just been revised and is

BOBOLINK

excellent, although somewhat highly priced at present. All three publications are well illustrated and especially compiled to assist in easy identification. They are available in paperback and hard cover.

A few words on correct wearing apparel might not be out of place. Wherever possible, wear subdued colours that blend with the background. Birds have excellent eyesight and hearing and are easily startled, so approach with caution. Too much emphasis cannot be placed on correct footwear. Many birds inhabit marshy areas, and in order to approach these birds at a close range, it may be necessary to get your feet wet. So waterproof boots are a must. ∾

BIRDWATCHING IN ALGONQUIN PARK

Not far distant from the populous centres of southern Ontario lies the wilderness haven of Algonquin Provincial Park. Here, in the land of lakes and forest, Ontario's oldest and, until Polar Bear Provincial Park was founded (in 1970), largest provincial park provides the ideal environment for many species of native birds.

FIELD SPARROW

Algonquin Park lies some 170 miles (274 km) northeast of Toronto, and is situated in the transitional zone. As such it acts as an intermediary between the northern Canadian (Boreal) and southern Carolinean zones. Many of our northern birds reach the southern limit of their range in the park and are rarely seen elsewhere in southern Ontario. Similarly, many southern species also reach their northern limit here.

The most attractive aspect of birding in Algonquin Park is that you do not have to roam the remote, inaccessible areas in order to see large numbers of birds as most forest-dwelling birds inhabit the edge of forests and open glades. Although each season sees the arrival of many species, perhaps the best birding may be expected during the early weeks of spring, reaching a peak in the first half of May. This is the time when many of our birds are returning from their tropical wintering grounds. By driving across the southern aspect of the park from west to

COMMON RAVEN

east along Highway 60, a stretch of almost 37 miles (60 km), you will find many species of birds.

The small, brightly coloured wood warblers may be the first species to attract your attention as they flit gaily from branch to branch, appearing to be almost in a state of perpetual motion. There are some 23 species of these birds to be found in the park at this time, when they are to be seen in their brightest breeding plumages. Among those certain to be encountered are the American Red-start (*Setophaga ruticilla*), Yellow-rumped Warbler (*Dendroica coronata*), Magnolia Warbler (*Dendroica magnolia*), Black-and-White Warbler (*Mniotilta varia*), Chestnut-sided Warbler (*Dendroica pensylvanica*), Palm Warbler (*Dendroica palmarum*), Cape May Warbler (*Dendroica tigrina*), and Northern Yellowthroat (*Geothlypis trichas*). It is essentially the males that are endowed with the most striking colouration; the females are positively drab by comparison.

COMMON LOON

The slightly larger and more sombre-looking vireos may also be seen in company with the warblers. Vireo, meaning literally "I am green", truly captures the general description of this family of birds. All are more or less a uniform olive-green and may, superficially at least, be mistaken for some species of female warblers. Vireos can be readily distinguished, however, by their more robust build and stouter bills and more leisurely and slower movements. The most common species is sure to be the Red-eyed Vireo (*Vireo olivaceus*), probably the most numerous species of breeding bird in eastern North America. Its distinguishing marks are a grey-blue head, white eye-stripe, and red iris from which it gets its name.

By now the swallows will have made their presence known and several kinds, usually Barn (*Hirundo rustica*), Bank (*Riparia riparia*), and Tree swallows (*Iridoprocne bicolor*), will be seen darting back and forth gathering insects stirred up by the highway activity. By many, these birds are considered the harbingers of spring for they are among the earliest species to return from the south. They are, however, usually preceded by Robins (*Turdus migratorius*), Red-winged Blackbirds (*Agelaius phoeniceus*), and White-throated Sparrows (*Zonotrichia albicollis*).

Somewhere along the highway you are certain to see a Common Raven (*Corvus corax*) or two perched in a tall yellow birch surveying the surrounding area, ever watchful for discarded food scraps or creatures killed by traffic. They are often accompanied by large numbers of Grey Jays (*Perisoreus canadensis*) also looking for handouts. These birds remain with us throughout the cold winter months and are perfectly well adapted to survive the extreme cold. The Grey Jay in particular is remarkable for it mates and produces its young usually in late winter in temperatures which may drop to 40° F below zero (−40° C).

OSPREY AND YOUNG

Most of Algonquin Park's larger lakes will have their pair or pairs of Common Loons (*Gavia immer*) cruising on the open water. These large, chequered black and white water birds are characteristic of the northern lakes, and their reverberating, yodelling calls are well-known to campers and canoeists in northern wilderness areas.

The Bald Eagle (*Haliaeetus leucocephalus*) and Osprey (*Pandion haliaetus*), both large fish-eating birds, had been sadly decreasing in numbers within recent years due to DDT poisoning and other pesticide residues absorbed by the fish on which they feed. This was especially so in the vicinity of the Great Lakes region where they became practically extinct. The cumulative effects of these poisons render the eggs infertile by affecting the calcium content in the birds' body. Happily, since the ban on DDT in 1972, there has been a definite upswing in their numbers. Although uncommon, it is still possible to see an occasional specimen of these birds in the park. Look for these birds over large areas of water. In the Algonquin environment there are records of fourteen species of hawks, but the Broad-winged Hawk (*Buteo platypterus*) is by far the most common. You will see this bird on the hydro and telephone wires waiting for a frog, snake, or mouse to show itself on the ground below.

Nine species of owls are recorded on the park's checklist, but the casual birdwatcher is likely to find only the Barred Owl (*Strix varia*). This is partly because of the forest cover. Mice and

40

GROUP OF BUNTINGS

other small mammals form a good deal of the food of these birds, and these are more easily obtained in open country. The Great Horned Owl (*Bubo virginianus*), generally thought of as a wilderness bird, is rare in the park.

A lively, high-pitched song, coming from the wires, will be an Indigo Bunting (*Passerina cyanea*), a small all-blue finch that nests in roadside shrubbery. Large numbers of Evening Grosbeaks (*Coccothraustes vespertina*) may be seen feeding on cone seeds along the highway. The Evening Grosbeak is a very colourful bird, especially the male. His plumage of yellow, black, brown, grey, and white in pronounced patches should identify this bird at once. His huge bill

has given him the descriptive name of "grosbeak".

You are sure to see a Great Blue Heron (*Ardea herodias*), the tallest bird in the park, fishing in a roadside marsh and occasionally taking flight on its five-foot (152 cm) wingspread, only to sail gracefully to another area of the marsh just a short distance away.

Algonquin Park is very well favoured in its numbers of woodpeckers, eight out of the possible nine eastern species having been recorded in the park. One spring I observed Pileated (*Dryocopus pileatus*), Downy (*Picoides pubescens*), Hairy (*Picoides villosus*), Yellow-bellied Sapsucker (*Sphyrapicus varius*), Common Flicker (*Colaptes auratus*), and Black-backed Three-toed Woodpecker (*Picoides arcticus*), and all from Highway 60. The Pileated Woodpecker is our largest and most handsome species and until recently exceedingly rare. Some forty years ago many authorities considered the bird to be in danger of extinction. However, since that time it has made a steady recovery. I had been birding for four years before I saw my first Pileated Woodpecker. What a magnifi-

cent sight! An almost crow-sized bird, glossy black and white with a flaming red crest. It was in the act of carving out a tree cavity prior to nesting and was so engrossed in its prenuptials I was able to observe it at close quarters.

I haven't really begun to mention the 220 or so bird species that have been recorded in the park, but it does give some idea of what Algonquin Park has to offer.

For further information regarding Algonquin Provincial Park write to:
Park Superintendent,
Ministry of Natural Resources,
Box 219,
Whitney, Ontario
K0J 2M0 ∼

41

SHRIKES

The Eastern Spiny Softshell Turtle (*Trionyx spiniferus*) is an odd-looking animal which is often referred to as "pancake" or "flapjack" because of the unusual shape and texture of its shell. Softshell turtles lack the usual hard protective shell or carapace which is characteristic of other turtles.

It has other unusual features, too — a long, snake-like neck, extensively webbed feet, and a tail that is so short it can barely be seen in some specimens. Its jaws are equipped with razor-sharp cutting edges concealed by fleshy lips, and have the power to inflict a very nasty injury, such as the biting off of a finger or two.

It is a fairly large species, growing up to fourteen inches (36 cm) long in Canada. Those in the United States tend to be larger; one has even been recorded at eighteen inches (46 cm). In colour, this turtle is variable — olive, greyish, or brown, with a white or pale yellow underside.

The softshell turtle is a swift, agile

IT LOOKS LIKE A PANCAKE

swimmer and is almost completely aquatic — hence, the webbed feet. It can stay under water for hours with only its snout above the surface. Occasionally, though, one may be seen sunbathing on the shore.

In Canada, this species has a very restricted range, being found mainly in the densely peopled areas of southern Ontario and Quebec. Unfortunately, its population is declining rapidly because of spreading urban development. In Quebec, it has been recorded at Ile Perrot, at the junction of the St. Lawrence and Ottawa rivers. It has also been recorded in the Pike River at the entrance to Mississquoi Bay, Lake Champlain. An old record from Ottawa was confirmed in more recent years by a sight record on the Ottawa River. In southern Ontario, this turtle is solely restricted to the western Lake Erie region.

Because of their rarity, softshell turtles should not be collected as pets. They are, in addition, ill adapted for this role because they are aggressive by nature, undoubtedly to compensate for the vulnerability of their soft shells.

The best means of saving this very unusual animal in Canada would be to make sure some of its deciduous forest habitat is conserved in southern Ontario and Quebec. ༕

1

Emergence of giant **Silk Moths** (*Saturniidae*).

5

Cassin's Kingbird (*Tyrannus vociferans*) collected from Algonquin Park, Ontario, 1953.

6

Gorgone Checkerspot Butterfly (*Chlosyne gorgone*) became extinct in Canada, 1891.

8

Black-throated Sparrow (*Amphispiza bilineata*) reported for Canada (Wells Gray Park, B.C.), 1959.

CALENDAR

9

Nest of **Hudsonian Godwit** (*Limosa haemastica*) discovered by Roderick Macfarlane in Mackenzie District, Northwest Territories, 1862.

15

150-year-old **Lake Sturgeon** (*Acipenser fulvescens*) caught in the Lake of the Woods, Ontario, 1953.

21

Sleepy Orange Sulphur Butterfly (*Eurema nicippe*) sighted in Canada (Quetico Park, Ontario), 1978.

23

Banff National Park founded, 1887.

29

Record for **Lake Sturgeon** (*Acipenser fulvescens*) from Batchewana Bay, Lake Superior (7 feet, 11 inches/241 cm, 310 lbs./141 kg), 1922.

30

Whooping Crane's (*Grus americana*) nesting area discovered (Wood Buffalo National Park), 1954.

TURTLES

Fourteen turtle species are native to Canada; ten of these are inland turtles, while four are marine species. Our species are, for the most part, confined to the southern parts of the provinces, although the Western Painted Turtle (*Chrysemys picta belli*) may be found as far north as La Pas in Manitoba.

Eastern Canada can boast of more turtle species than the west, and the Point Pelee region of southwestern Ontario probably plays host to more turtle species than are found anywhere else in Canada. As in the case of the snakes, there are no inland native turtles in Newfoundland, and no native species that are not also represented in the United States.

Turtles are unique by virtue of their hard shell, which is divided into two parts. The upper part is known as the "carapace", the lower the "plastron", and in most species these two parts are joined on each side by a bridge. The sections of the carapace and plastron are called "scutes" or plates.

It is known that turtles have been on the earth for a long time, as fossil remains date back about 200 million years when the reptiles were the dominant animals on earth. The ancestor of modern-day turtles is not known, but it is believed that these animals derive from a primitive lizard-like reptile called the "Cotylosaur".

In Canada and the northern United States, turtles hibernate below the frost line in order to escape freezing during the long, cold winters. Terrestrial species seek out mammal burrows, debris, and old stump holes, while aquatic species spend the winter under mud at the bottom of bodies of water.

The Snapping Turtle (*Chelydra serpentina serpentina*) is Canada's largest species, and may attain a carapace length of more than seventeen inches (43 cm) and weigh more than fifty pounds (22 kg). However, this species fares badly in comparison with the Alligator Snapping Turtle (*Macroclemys temmincki*), which is one of the giants of all freshwater turtles, and can weigh as much as 200 pounds (90 kg). The last-mentioned is the largest species to be found in the southern United States.

Our smallest freshwater turtles are the

SNAPPING TURTLE

Spotted Turtle (*Clemmys guttata*) and the Common Musk Turtle or Stinkpot (*Sternotherus odoratus*), both with a carapace length of between three and five inches (7.5 to 13 cm), and both restricted in Canada to southern Ontario.

The Leatherback Turtle (*Dermochelys coriacea*) has the distinction of being the world's largest sea turtle, and can attain a weight of 2,000 pounds (900 kg). The Pacific Leatherback Turtle (*D.c. schegeli*) has been found off the coast of Vancouver Island, and off the

southern tip of the Queen Charlotte Islands, British Columbia. In 1934, a specimen weighing 1,200 pounds (545 kg) was caught in a fisherman's net off Nootka Island. The Atlantic Leatherback Turtle (*D.c. coriacea*) has been sighted in the waters off the coast of Newfoundland, Nova Scotia, Cape Breton Island, New Brunswick, and Prince Edward Island.

Turtles are generally noted for their longevity, and the giant Galapagos Tortoise is known to live for about 150 years,

LEATHERBACK TURTLE

BLANDING'S TURTLE

while our Eastern Box Turtle (*Terrapene carolina carolina*) may live for 138 years. The Musk Turtle of Ontario has a longevity record of 53 years. In scientific classification, very little distinction is made between turtles, terrapins, and tortoises, though generally the more aquatic species are referred to as turtles, the land-dwelling, high-domed carapace species as tortoises, and small edible aquatic species as terrapins (i.e. the Diamond-back Terrapins [*Malaclemys sp.*] of the United States). Of the 250 species of turtles remaining in the world today, more than forty forms are

STINKPOT

listed as "threatened" or "endangered" by the Survival Service Commission, International Union for Conservation of Nature and Natural Resources.

Like lizards, salamanders have the ability to snap off their tails, when grasped by this appendage. The animal appears to be in no way incapacitated and there is little or no blood. It will soon grow a new tail, not quite as long as the original one, but just as useful. Salamanders are also able to change their colour somewhat, usually to a darker shade.∿

PAINTED TERRAPIN

Salamanders belong to the amphibian order "*Urodela*" and, though similar in appearance to lizards, have neither claws nor scales, and have no more than four toes as compared to the lizard's five. Salamanders vary tremendously in size, some no bigger than a small earthworm, while there is one, the Giant Salamander (*Megalobatrarchus maximus*), from Japan which attains a length of over five feet (150 cm). North America is especially rich in salamanders; the number of native species is given at 135, greater than the number distributed throughout the rest of the world. Canada's contribution to the salamander count, however, amounts to only twenty species.

The old belief that salamanders had the power to endure fire without harm

salamanders remain immature throughout their lives as in the case of the Mudpuppy (*Necturus maculosus*) and a form of Tiger Salamander from Mexico which do not pass to the adult stage although, of course, they are able to breed.

Such amphibians (known as "*neotenous*") never lose their external gills; they may develop lungs but still retain their gills. Most of them are born in water and remain there throughout their lives. The cause of this neotenousness is the thyroid gland, the chief regulator of metamorphosis. Laboratory experiments have shown that when non-neotenous salamander larvae are injected with extracts from the thyroid of neotenous salamanders, there is an immediate transformation to the adult stage.

SPOTTED SALAMANDER

was current in biblical times. In fact, the myth was exploded nearly 2,000 years ago — in his natural history, the elder Pliny (A.D. 23-79) tells us of an experiment in which a salamander was put into fire, and as expected, was burnt to a powder. The name of these animals, derived from the Greek meaning "fire animal", is a misnomer indeed, as the salamander shuns heat and requires a great deal of moisture in order to live.

Salamanders lay jelly-covered eggs, usually in water. The larvae maintain external gills throughout their larval life, and lose them when they gradually transform into adult salamanders. Some

Both as a larva and as an adult, the salamander is carnivorous and consumes great quantities of insects of all varieties, in addition to worms. The larger species will even eat frogs and smaller salamanders. In turn, salamanders have many enemies, but there are a number of ways in which these amphibians are able to defend themselves. Probably the most valuable protection they possess is the skin which becomes lubricated and makes the salamander slippery and difficult to catch. In some salamanders there is the added protection of the granular glands which can exude an evil-smelling secretion. Also, there are the teeth which are often slanted back towards the throat making it difficult for food and enemies to wriggle free from their grasp.

Salamanders are found almost entirely in the north temperate regions, with virtually none south of the equator. They are in fact able to exist anywhere in temperate climates, except in extreme regions like arctic wastes and high mountain peaks.

In North America very little distinction is made between newts and salamanders; newts are generally considered as being just a type of salamander. Superficially, newts and salamanders are very much alike. Newts are more confined to an aquatic life, and are sometimes called "water-salamanders". Also, a newt has a slimmer body than a salamander, terminating in a strongly compressed tail, whereas that of a salamander is rounded. Finally, newts but not salamanders shed their skin periodically. The old one begins to break at the mouth and is peeled away from the body in one piece.

Some of the more familiar native salamanders include: Tiger Salamander (*Ambystoma tigrinum*), Spotted Salamander (*Ambystoma maculatum*), Jefferson Salamander (*Ambystoma jeffersonianum*), and Long-tailed Salamander (*Eurycea longicauda*). The Northern Red Salamander (*Pseudotriton ruber ruber*), the rarest salamander in Canada, may not be a native to this country at all, but may have appeared here by accident from the United States. There have been one or two unofficial sightings from Ontario, but only one positive identification, from Dunchurch, near Parry Sound, in 1946. ∽

⇒ INSECT MUSICIANS ⇐

The Short-horned Grasshoppers, or Locusts, make a rasping sound by rubbing their hind legs against their front wings. When at rest, the true wings are folded like a fan underneath the front wings. There are rows of tiny pegs on the hind legs and when these are scraped against the rough wings, the resulting

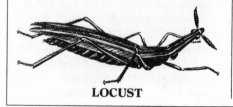

LOCUST

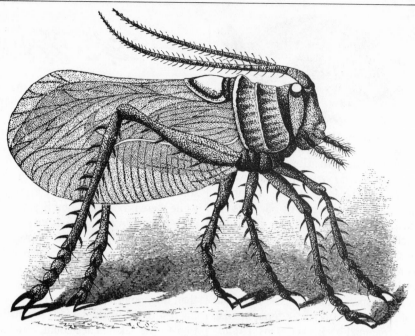

KATYDID

sound is much like that made by scraping the teeth of a comb across the thumbnail. Certain Short-horned Grasshoppers have gaily coloured hind wings and these are displayed in flight by rapid opening and closing, producing a sound that has given them the name of "castanet grasshoppers".

The sound-producing apparatus of the Long-horned Grasshoppers and Katydids is quite different from that of their short-horned relatives. Male Long-horns "fiddle" by rubbing the underside of one wing on the other. A file-like ridge on one wing rubs against a rough area on the other, the wings themselves acting as sounding boards and producing the familiar high-pitched chirping.

Katydids are bright green, almost transparent, insects that live in trees and so are seldom seen, although their music is loud and clear. By drawing a "bow" on the left wing across a "string" on the right, they produce a noise that sounds a little like "Katy did, she didn't, she did" from which they get their name.

Crickets are perhaps the best known insect musicians, and many species contribute to the ensemble. As with most insects, their activities rise and fall with the temperature, and a reasonably accurate estimate of the Fahrenheit temperature may be obtained by counting the number of chirps for a specified period, and adding a number that varies with the species of cricket. The formula for the Field Cricket (*Gryllus sp.*) is the number of chirps in 14 seconds plus 40. ∽

THE DIFFERENCE BETWEEN BUTTERFLIES AND MOTHS

The most obvious difference between moths and butterflies is in the formation of their antennae, or feelers. Butterflies, which form the suborder *Rhopalocera*, meaning "club-tipped", have club-like knobs on the end of their antennae; whereas moths, in the sub-order *Heterocera*, have antennae of various kinds. They may be feathered or fern-like (pectinated) like those of the Silk Moths (*Saturniidae*), or smooth and tapering with a hook tip like those of the Sphinx Moths (*Sphingiidae*). Never are their antennae clubbed, however.

There are other differences, not quite so specific. The bodies of butterflies are generally much slimmer, and divided into three quite distinct parts: head, chest (thorax), and abdomen. The bodies

RED ADMIRAL BUTTERFLY

of moths are usually stout, with the head and thorax less defined and merging into one part. When resting, butterflies usually fold their wings together above their heads, showing their undersides. Moths usually rest with their wings spread out. Butterflies fly during the day, whereas most moths fly during evening or night.

However, there are some moths that fly in broad daylight, and very occasionally the Red Admiral Butterfly (*Vanessa atalanta*) has been found flying to light with the nocturnal moths. It is generally supposed by laymen that all butterflies are brilliantly coloured while moths are drab and dingy. But there are many moths, of the tropical day-flying species, that can rival any butterfly for sheer brilliance of colour, while some butterflies are quite plain.

Butterflies and moths together form the order *Lepidoptera*, meaning "scaly-winged". The wings of butterflies and moths are composed of millions of tiny scales, formed rather like the tiles on a roof. ∾

HOG SPHINX MOTH

✕SWALLOWTAIL✕ BUTTERFLIES

HUDSONIAN SWALLOWTAIL

tails recorded from Canada, the Tiger Swallowtail (*Papilio glaucus*) and the Black Swallowtail (*P. polyxenes asterias*) are perhaps the best-known and most frequently encountered.

Strong, sailing flight and an addiction to garden flowers bring the Tiger Swallowtail into large cities, although it is generally a butterfly of the woodlands. The butterfly that is seen by most Canadians is the northern subspecies, the Canadian Tiger Swallowtail (*P.g. canadensis*), which is smaller and slightly paler than the typical form. This is the large yellow and black butterfly that one sees regularly in cottage country during late May and early June. Males of this species will often congregate at mud puddles in the early morning and again in the evening. The name "*glaucus*" (dull greyish) refers to the dark female form that is found regularly in the southern United States. The larva of this species is green, when fully grown, with false eye-spots, so that the animal resembles the head of a small green snake. This colour pattern is believed to deter predators.

The handsome Black Swallowtail is a very widespread eastern species of the fields and roadsides, but, like the Tiger Swallowtail, it can also be found on garden flowers. As its name suggests, this butterfly is largely black with yellow spots and blue along the border of the hind wings. The yellow spots are fewer but the blue colouration is more pronounced in the females, who also tend to be larger. Young larvae resemble bird droppings; older ones are green with black bands containing yellow spots. They feed on leaves of the parsley family, both wild and cultivated, and are sometimes a pest in vegetable gardens where parsley, celery, carrots, and parsnips are raised.

Both species are absent from the far west where they are replaced respectively by the Western Tiger Swallowtail (*Papilio rutulus*) and the Anise Swallowtail (*P. zelicaon*). ∾

TAWNY EMPEROR

The Swallowtail family includes the largest and most colourful of Canada's butterflies. Consequently, they are the species most often noticed by non-naturalists because of their striking appearance.

The larvae (caterpillars) of this family of butterfly are often brightly coloured and have scent glands which are raised in the form of orange horns when the caterpillars are threatened. These scent glands or "osmeteria" give out a strong musky odour and probably act as a defence against predators.

The butterflies tend to be large and have tail-like projections on their hind wings, hence their name. In more tropical climes, though, some Swallowtails are tailless.

Of the fourteen species of Swallow-

47

UNUSUAL CATERPILLARS

TWIN-SPOTTED SPHINX MOTH

TIGER MOTH

Some moths have very odd-looking caterpillars. One such species is the Puss Moth (*Cerura vinula*), a large member of the "prominents". The caterpillar's hind legs are formed into long whiplashes which it extends and beats about in the air when disturbed. At the same time, it appears to puff itself up and raise the front end of its body. By so doing, it looks like the head of a much larger animal, and probably obtains some protection by frightening off or greatly discouraging potential attackers. Its colouration is of the type known as "disruptive" — the pattern consists of bold, irregular patches of contrasting tones which disguise the caterpillar by apparently breaking up its shape into two or more separate objects.

One very common native species, the Isabella Tiger Moth (*Isia isabella*), has a very furry caterpillar of rich chestnut-brown with black at both ends. It is an especially common sight in the fall to see these "woolly bears" hurrying across the roads or paths looking for a place to spin their cocoons. The caterpillar is falsely reputed to have the ability to forecast the weather. A common superstition holds that if the black ends are longer than usual the following winter will be a hard one. Needless to say, there is no scientific basis for this belief.

Caterpillars of the Hawk Moths or *Sphingidae* are characterized by having horn-like protuberances at the ends of their abdomens. In some cases the horn is replaced by a tubercle. Hawk Moth caterpillars will often rest with their heads and bodies raised in a somewhat sphinx-like position, hence the name "*Sphingidae*". They are usually of various shades of green, thereby matching the leaves among and on which they feed, and often they have diagonal markings that simulate the veins of the leaves. In spite of the impressive size of Hawk Moth caterpillars (up to five or six inches [13 to 15 cm] in some species) they are usually difficult to locate because of their protective colouration. ᴖ

SEMBLING

Many of our largest and most attractive moths have proven to be easy to breed in captivity. A popular method of rearing giant silk moths, known as "sembling", involves the use of a captive female specimen to attract males of the species.

In this method, a recently emerged female moth, such as a Cecropia (*Hyalophora cecropia*), has a thin thread fastened to its abdomen; the other end of the thread is attached to a piece of screening which is hung up in a tree. The screen with the attached female should be hung out in the late afternoon and allowed to remain through the night.

The tethered female broadcasts her existence through her mating odours, thereby attracting large numbers of eligible males in the general vicinity. Under ideal conditions, the scent of the female can reach males fully a mile away. ᴖ

THE DEFENSIVE CIRCLE

The Muskox (*Ovibos moschatus*) was first described by Henry Kelsey of the Hudson's Bay Company while he was exploring that region on June 17, 1689:

"Two Buffilo...ill shapen beast. Their body being bigger than an ox... their horns not growing like other Beast but joyn together upon their forehead and so come down ye side of their head and turn up till ye tip be even with ye side of their head and turn up till ye tip be even with ye Buts. Their Hair is near a foot long."

It confounded early scientists in 1780 when they named it *"Ovibos moschatus"*, literally, "musky sheep-cow". But, it is neither; nor is it closely related to either of these animals. In fact, its closest (and still rather distant) living relative is the Takin of Tibet, Burma, and China.

Muskoxen were numerous for a century after Kelsey's discovery. Samuel Hearne recording sighting a herd while trekking from Hudson Bay to the Arctic Ocean: "Saw many herds of them in the course of a day's walk, and some of those herds did not contain less than eighty or a hundred head."

MUSKOX

Apart from man, the main enemy of the muskox is the wolf. When faced with an attack of wolves, the muskoxen line up in "hedgehog formation", a circle or semicircle, with the calves and immature animals in the centre. The adults face outwards, their sharp and sweeping horns towards the enemy. Should a wolf approach too closely, an adult muskox will rush out and try to gore it before returning to the defensive circle. This most effective defensive stratagem usually means triumph over a pack of wolves and suicide against a man with a gun.

WOLF

> **"** There are, of course, several things in Ontario that are more dangerous than wolves. For instance, the step-ladder. **"**
>
> *J. W. Curran*

The Common Opossum (*Didelphis virginiana*) can claim three distinctions in the annals of wildlife lore: its family *Didelphidae* dates back to Cretaceous times, making it one of the oldest of living mammalian families; it is the only marsupial that occurs north of Mexico; and its method of self-defence, "playing possum", has been adopted with varying success by humans.

CARDINAL AND ROSE-BREASTED GROSBEAK

When it hovers over a flower, a hummingbird's wings can hardly be seen because they are beating at an incredible 55 beats per second. This gives it all the manoeuvrability of a helicopter, enabling it to hang suspended in mid-air, fly backwards, dart sideways, and rise vertically.

But this is nothing when compared with the beating rate it achieves when flying at a speed of 60 miles an hour (97 km/h), which it does often. Its wings then vibrate about 200 times a second. The hummingbird's top speed is said to be 80 miles an hour (129 km/h), attained when it is chasing another hummingbird. It can keep up a speed of 60 miles an hour (97 km/h) for hundreds of miles without a stop. During the migration north from Central

HIGH MANOEUVRABILITY

America in spring, Ruby-throated Hummingbirds (*Archilochus colubris*) fre-

quently pass ships 200 miles (322 km) out at sea, travelling four or five times faster than the ships.

Hummingbirds are also especially pugnacious, and will attack birds much larger than themselves. They have been known to engage hawks and eagles in aerial combat. Their weapon is their long, needle-like bill which they use to attack the eyes of their enemies, and this, coupled with their ability to fly straight up, down, sideways, and backwards, makes them a very dangerous adversary.

Not surprisingly, hummingbirds have the highest energy output per unit of weight of any living warm-blooded animal. They also have the lowest blood temperature: readings as low as 56°F (13.3°C) have been recorded. ∾

1

International Trade in Endangered Fauna & Flora came into force, 1975.

4

Xerces Society's Annual Butterfly Count.

5

Last recorded **Great Auk** (*Penguinus impennis*) in North America (Funk Island, Newfoundland), 1785. First **Giant Beaked Whale** (*Berardius bairdi*) in Canadian waters (Quatsino Sound, B.C.), 1950.

CALENDAR

18

Crested **Caracara** (*Polyborus plancus*) in Canada (Port Arthur, Ontario), 1892. John Macoun, Canadian naturalist, died, 1920.

20

Black Witch Moth (*Erebus odora*) captured in Canada (near Sarnia, Ontario), 1968.

21

Arctic Warbler (*Phylloscopus borealis*) reported for Canada (Prince Patrick Island, N.W.T.), 1949.

29

The First Almanac, 1457.

> **⌐ Farmer's Calendar ⌐**
> With July in the North come most roses, blossoms on chestnut sprouts, ripe strawberries early in the month, and orange wood lilies and blueberries before the month is over in the more northern areas.
> Sow second crops of quick growers like beans, beets, carrots, and late crops like Chinese cabbage. Cut out old raspberry and blackberry stems as soon as the main fruiting is over even on everbearing sorts.
> Clean up and destroy rust-infected hollyhock leaves and spray those remaining with any good fungicide. Divide and replant overcrowded iris

THE TIME IT RAINED BLOOD

In July 1608, the neighbourhood of Aix-en-France was covered with red patches, which led to a general belief that it had rained blood. Fortunately, a man more intelligent than his neighbours had been keeping a butterfly chrysalis in a box. Hearing a noise inside he opened the box and a butterfly flew out, leaving behind it the empty chrysalis and a red stain (the fluids a butterfly emits during its emergence), which proved to be identical with the supposed spots of blood which had caused his neighbours so much alarm. The man was then able to demonstrate to his neighbours' satisfaction that the red patches were simply due to the abundance of butterflies at that particular season. ∾

THE NEAR-FISHES

The most primitive vertebrates are lampreys and Hagfish (*Myxine glutinosa*). They belong to a group of animals, the *Cyclostomata*, which resembles fish except that the members of this group have no jaws.

They are characterized by a row of gill pouches, used for respiration, down each side of the body, just behind the head. Both lampreys and hagfish have eel-like bodies covered by a layer of slime and a single fin near the tail.

They are a very ancient form of life; fossils have been found which are thought to be the ancient representatives of the group that lived about 400 million years ago.

Lampreys are found throughout the world and have long been used as food by man. The Romans kept them alive in tanks and served them as delicacies, and old records tell us they were sold at fairs and markets in Great Britain. King Henry I of England was popularly thought to have died from a surfeit of them.

Lampreys have no jaws, and the mouth is a large circular funnel-shaped sucker situated at the end of the head. The sucker and tongue are set with a number of sharp horny protuberances which resemble teeth but have a different structure from the true teeth of fish.

Lampreys feed by attaching themselves to their prey, usually fish, by means of the sucker and then sucking the blood and rasping the flesh off their victim by moving their tongues backwards and forwards. They cause great destruction in shoals of fishes and fishermen regard them as dangerous pests. ∾

Fish are ideally equipped for their existence in water. Their tails are adapted in the same way as sculling oars for propelling their streamlined bodies through the water. They have fins to help maintain their balance and direction, and are also equipped with swim bladders which make it possible for them to go up and down as they please. By expelling gases out of their swim bladders they are able to sink; forcing gases in again from the bloodstream enables them to rise.

There are many varieties of fish of different shapes and forms. A typical fish has two pairs of fins, corresponding to the limbs of four-footed mammals; these are known as the pectoral and ventral fins. Also, there is usually a single prominent fin situated on the back (the dorsal fin), and the tail fin itself (the caudal fin).

Fish, unlike mammals and birds, continue to grow throughout their lifetime: the older the fish the greater its size. However, fish do vary greatly in size according to their environment. Those inhabiting large bodies of water, such as lakes and rivers, tend to be distinctly greater in size than the same species found in small ponds and brooks. The amount of available food in the water also has a decided bearing on their size.

Fish breathe by way of gills situated at the back of the head and protected by gill covers. Incidentally, almost all fish have ears of a kind, but they are hidden. It is generally believed that fish make little use of their hearing, but rely more on their sense of smell to seek out their food.

Young fish feed on plankton (minute plant and animal life), while most adults feed on smaller fish species and other vertebrate animals. Some fish, however, are strictly plant eaters. Fish are also an important source of food for many other animals. Their only means of protection is their ability to hide and to swim fast. Very young fish are almost entirely defenceless, and the chances of most of them reaching maturity are extremely slim. That is why many species lay millions of eggs at one time.

Fish and fisheries constitute a valuable part of Canada's natural resources, for not only are they of considerable commercial value, but they are also of importance as a form of outdoor recreation. Although relatively rich in supplies of fresh water, Canada is not rich in fish species, and most fish found here also occur in the United States. However, from a fisherman's viewpoint, what Canada lacks in quantity is compensated for in quality. This country has some of the finest salmon, trout, and char populations available anywhere, although industrial development and technological fallout are threatening the continued existence of those species even in the most remote places.

Here are just a few of the popular fish species to be found in the inland waters of Canada:

RAINBOW TROUT
(SALMO GAIRDNERI)

The very attractive Rainbow Trout is originally a native of the Pacific coastal waters of North America and was introduced into the Canadian lakes at the early part of the century. It has the typically trout-shaped, laterally compressed body and a large mouth with many large teeth. There are variations in colour and body form, which are generally believed to be environmentally controlled. Taxonomists conclude that if all the various forms were placed together in the same environment, they would become quite indistinguishable from one another.

The Rainbow Trout has a distinctive vivid red or purplish broad band which extends from behind the eye across the body and tail. This coloured band is only evident in adult fish, especially in spawning males. It is from this feature that the fish gets its name. Its back is green or greenish-blue, blending to silvery on the sides, while the underside is white. Numerous black spots also adorn the top of the head, the body, and the fins.

Maturity generally takes two to three years, and spawning usually takes place about April or May, with the adults migrating upstream to clear rapid water. There, a nest is constructed in the clean gravel. With the completion of spawning, the adults move downstream again, where they usually remain permanently. The Rainbow is an exceptionally popular game fish because of its fighting ability and its beauty.

The size of Rainbow Trout varies greatly with the type of habitat: Great Lakes trout grow to about 36 inches (91 cm) and weigh up to 20 pounds (9 kg), while those in Newfoundland usually attain a weight of only 7.5 pounds (3 kg). Pacific Ocean specimens tend to be the largest of all, and the record catch for this species may be one taken many years ago in Jewel Lake in British Columbia which tipped the scales at 52 pounds (24 kg).

BROOK TROUT

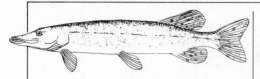

NORTHERN PIKE
(ESOX LUCIUS)

The Northern Pike is found throughout most of Europe and Northern Asia as well as North America. It ranges throughout the entire northern part of our continent south to Missouri, where it is easily identified by its very elongated and somewhat compressed body. The head is large, as is the mouth with its many long, needle-sharp teeth. This species may be readily distinguished from the closely related Muskellunge (*Esox masquinongy*) by its different arrangement of markings and colouration, and by the less extensive scaling on its cheeks.

The ground colour consists of various shades of green, graduating to lighter hues on the sides. There are also numerous light horizontal spots along the sides and dark green blotching on the yellowish fins. The underneath is white. Very young pike have light vertical bars.

Spawning takes place in the early spring in shallow bays and marshy areas, and they return to spawn in the same area every year. In summer, pike can be found in weedy shallows of lakes hanging motionless just below the surface of the water. They move into deeper water with the onset of winter.

The Northern Pike is one of our most popular fish, and is of high commercial importance, especially in our northern inland waters. They feed primarily on other fish, such as Yellow Perch, minnows, and suckers, and supplement their diet occasionally with frogs, snakes, mice, small ducks, and muskrats.

These fish may grow to a large size: specimens measuring over three feet (91 cm) in length and weighing over twenty pounds (9 kg) are not uncommon. Pike are considered to grow much larger in Europe than in North American, however; a list of large British pike drawn up in 1971 included at least eight individuals that equal or exceed all North American records. The angler record for a pike in Canada is often cited as one caught in Stoney Rapids, Saskatchewan, in 1954, which weighed 42 pounds 12 ounces (19 kg).

LARGEMOUTH BASS
(MICROPTERUS SALMOIDES)

The Largemouth Bass is a large, deep-bodied fish, which is distinguished from the similar Smallmouth Bass (*Micropterus dolomieui*) by the larger mouth which extends beyond the eye. The fins are not so uniform in length, and the dorsal fin is very deeply notched. The Largemouth also has a broader, more powerful tail.

It is usually dark green on its back, shading to a lighter green on its side, with the underside being of a light colour. There is a broad dark band of irregular patches on the sides which is more distinctive in younger fish.

Spawning occurs in early May in warm weedy waters. However, it is very adaptable and is found in many different types of localities. Before spawning, the male chooses a nesting site which consists of a depression in the muddy bottom. The eggs and young are actively protected for a while by the male fish before it abandons them and allows them to fend for themselves.

This species is somewhat cannibalistic, with some specimens eating smaller members of their own kind. Their diet usually consists of other fish species, especially minnows, crayfish, and frogs. Feeding is usually conducted in the morning and evening, while they roam near the surface at twilight and move to deeper water during the day.

This is one of the most popular of game fish, and generally tends to be larger than the Smallmouth Bass. A large specimen may weigh between six and eight pounds (3 to 4 kg), and measure seven to ten inches (18 to 25 cm) in length. The present known maximum size for a Largemouth Bass in Canada is an individual of 14 pounds 2 ounces (6 kg) caught in Stoney Lake, Peterborough County, Ontario, in 1948.

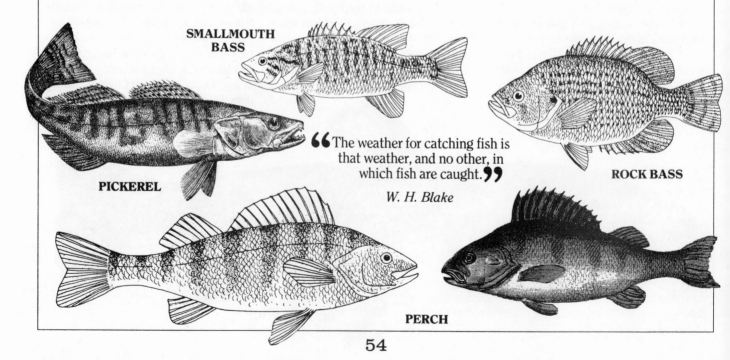

SMALLMOUTH BASS

PICKEREL

ROCK BASS

PERCH

"The weather for catching fish is that weather, and no other, in which fish are caught.**"**

W. H. Blake

54

YELLOW PERCH
(PERCA FLAVESCENS)

The Yellow Perch is represented in Europe as well as North America. It is found in every province of Canada although it is far more common in the northern and eastern areas. The young of this species are preyed on by almost all other predatory fish such as Bass, Sunfish, Crappies, Walleye (*Stizostedion vitreum*), Sauger (*Stizostedion canadense*), Northern Pike, Muskellunge, Lake Trout, and even other Yellow Perch. In the same way, the adults are prey for many species of water birds. The principal diet of the perch is animal plankton, aquatic insects, and other small fish, especially minnows and sticklebacks.

This fish is generally an olive-green colour, graduating to yellow on the sides. There are six to eight broad, dark vertical crossbars running down the sides. The belly is pale, generally whitish or yellowish, and the very distinctive upper fins are separated and somewhat dusky in colour.

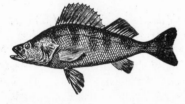

It generally takes two years for the Yellow Perch to attain sexual maturity, at which time spawning usually occurs at night during April and May, in shallow, sheltered areas. The eggs are embedded in a gelatinous covering and hatch in approximately three weeks. No parental care is given to the young fish.

Yellow Perch tend to be more numerous where there are expanses of open water with a moderate amount of vegetation, especially in warmer waters. They are very gregarious and usually travel about in large shoals. Essentially fish of larger lakes, they are often found in small bodies of water as well.

Yellow Perch caught by anglers in Canada are usually eight to twelve inches (20 to 30 cm) long, and weigh between four and ten ounces (113 to 283 g). However, a fourteen-inch (36 cm) perch was taken in the Saugeen River (Lake Huron), Ontario, in 1929, and one weighing 4 pounds 1 ounce (1.9 kg) was caught in Quebec.

LAKE STURGEON
(ACIPENSER FULVESCENS)

The Lake Sturgeon is one of our largest fish and also our most primitive, retaining the cartilaginous skeleton of the earliest fish. Its elongated, almost cylindrical body tapers towards the tail. There are a number of bony plates along its back which are more prominent in younger fish. The snout is long and pointed, and there are only four barbels in front of the mouth which assist the fish in locating its prey.

In Canada, the Lake Sturgeon is widespread throughout the eastern provinces. The general colouration of adult sturgeons is predominently slate-grey, varying to dark-grey, black, and even green. It is a denizen of lakes and large rivers, where it is long-lived and takes many years to reach maturity.

Large females may produce upwards of 500,000 eggs at a single spawning. The very young fish feed on minute crustaceans, moving on to mayfly nymphs as they get a little older. They are especially useful in outdoor ponds as they help considerably in keeping down the amount of algae that collect there.

Before the Lake Sturgeon was recognized as a desirable food fish it was indiscriminately destroyed by fishermen because it often became entangled in their nets and ripped great holes in them. As sturgeon eggs produce the highly desirable caviar which commands such a high price on the market, commercial fishing is now strictly regulated by the government.

In the Great Lakes area, Lake Sturgeon may occasionally take on enormous proportions, sometimes attaining a weight of 300 pounds (136 kg) and measuring seven feet in length (213 cm). Fish of this size, however, are now exceedingly rare. Apparently the largest Lake Sturgeon recorded weighed 310 pounds (141 kg), was 7 feet 11 inches long (241 cm), and was caught in Batchewana Bay, Lake Superior, Ontario, on June 29, 1922.

PUMPKINSEED
(LEPOMIS GIBBOSUS)

The Pumpkinseed is the most common and most widely distributed of our native sunfish. It is distinctly rounder than other members of the family and is quite unmistakeable. The body is covered with large scales of many colours. No other species of freshwater fish exhibits such a great variety of colours and markings. The back is generally greenish, graduating to blue with orange or rust spots on the side, and the cheeks are orange with wavy brilliant blue streaks which are more highly coloured in the male. Mature females have distinct vertical bars.

It is partial to warm-water, heavily weeded areas where there is abundant food and enough shelter in which to hide from its enemies. Spawning takes place quite late, generally in June or July. Like all sunfishes, the male Pumpkinseed is very aggressive at spawning time. It constructs the nest and possessively stands guard over the newly hatched young, chasing away all intruders.

The Pumpkinseed has a prolific reproduction potential, sometimes becoming too numerous for the available food supply. The fish then become stunted in size, rarely attaining lengths of more than four to five inches (10 to 13 cm) under such circumstances. Under optimum conditions lengths of eight to nine inches (20 to 23 cm) are not unusual, and a length of ten inches (25 cm) and weight of seventeen ounces (482 g) would appear to be the maximum size for this species in Canada. Because of their size they are usually ignored by the adult angler, although their flesh is sweet and of excellent flavour.

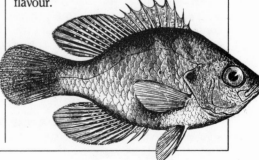

CARP
(CYPRINUS CARPIO)

The Carp is not indigenous to North America, but is an introduced species. Closely related to the popular domesticated Goldfish (*Carassius auratus*), it was originally a native of Asia. It was first introduced into Europe by way of Cyprus, early in the Middle Ages, but did not reach North America until around 1877. It is now widely distributed throughout the entire eastern part of the continent.

These fish have very robust bodies furnished with many large, overlapping scales, and moderate-sized mouths which are toothless with slightly protruding upper jaws. There is also a pair of conspicuous barbels situated at the corner of the mouth. The ground colour of the adult fish ranges from olive-green on its back to yellowish on its belly. The lower half of the caudal and anal fins has a distinct reddish hue.

Spawning commences in late spring sometimes extending into late summer, usually in shallow, heavily weeded waters. There is much violent activity at this time; the thrashings of some of these spawning Carp frequently cause them to leap clear of the water.

Carp are gregarious fish, generally moving around in large shoals in warm, shallow waters of lakes and rivers, and stirring up a great deal of mud at the bottom. They are extremely hardy and able to tolerate dry conditions better than most other fish. With the approach of winter, they move into deeper water, returning again to the more shallow waters in the spring.

These fish can grow to an incredible size; giants of up to 40 pounds (18 kg) are not unheard of and it is on record that a specimen weighing 86 pounds (39 kg) was caught in Minnesota in 1906. Possibly the largest Carp taken in Canada was a 39-pound (17.7 kg) fish caught in a poundnet near Port Dover on Lake Erie in Ontario.

THE PREACHER BIRD

Vireos are small passerine birds that are in many ways superficially similar to the warblers. The word "vireo" — "I am green" — is an apt name for these olive-backed birds with white underparts tinged with yellow or grey. Some vireos have wingbars, some do not. Most have eye-rings with a connecting band, giving them a somewhat spectacled look. They are best distinguished from warblers by their thicker, slightly hooked bills and slower, more deliberate movements; they are far less fluttery and active than warblers.

**BLACK-THROATED
GREEN WARBLER**

By far the most familiar bird of the family is the Red-eyed Vireo (*Vireo olivaceus*) which is generally regarded as the most abundant nesting bird of the eastern deciduous forests of North America. Its distinctive features are the red iris, prominent eye stripe, and blue-grey cap. The Red-eyed Vireo has earned for itself the nickname of "Preacher Bird" which derives from the monotonous repetition of its song. One male is reported to have repeated its refrain 22,197 times between dawn and dusk, a record not likely to be challenged except by another Red-eyed Vireo.

RED-EYED VIREO

A PARASITE

Nobody has ever found a nest of the Brown-headed Cowbird (*Molothrus ater*), because it does not have one. It is the only entirely parasitic North American bird, taking the place here of the cuckoo in Europe which also lays its eggs in the nests of other birds.

The species gets its name from its habit of following cattle about the fields in order to take advantage of the insects stirred up by the feeding animals. In the old days they were called "Buffalo Birds" because they followed the bison herds, and the suggestion has been made that they lost their nest-building habit by following the moving herds and not staying long enough in one place to make a nest.

Before we knew much about such things it was thought that cowbirds were complete gypsies, wandering around the country and laying eggs in other nests at random. It is now known, however, that they pair as other birds do, and claim a certain territory, within which the female lays about five eggs in various nests. Their unwilling hosts are usually the smaller birds, such as sparrows, warblers, and vireos. The eggs are sneaked in when the rightful owners are absent, and most of these never notice the difference. Even when the aggressive young cowbird takes more than its share of the food, or pushes its smaller nest-mates out of the nest, the deluded foster parents go right on feeding it.

Nobody loves a parasite, and the cowbird is often considered to be a most undesirable bird. The modern student of zoology, however, is inclined to allow that it has its place in nature. It is a fact that two of the birds it most often imposes on, the Song Sparrow (*Melospiza melodia*) and the Red-eyed Vireo (*Vireo olivaceus*), are among our most abundant species.

THE ELUSIVE MOLE

AMERICAN SHREW MOLE

There are few people who could not count the number of times they have seen a live mole, although we walk over their underground homes every day.

The only signs we see of their presence are little mounds of earth or, quite often, low ridges on the surface. The mounds are made of earth pushed up from their permanent burrows, which may be two feet (61 cm) from the surface; the ridges are simply displaced soil heaved up by the animal's body as it goes from one place to another. Trying to find a mole, even where there are many surface signs, and even if you use a shovel, is generally difficult. Moles make their nests and spend most of their time far below the reach of surface excavations. For this reason there are many details of mole life history still not well known to mammalogists.

Although they cause annoyance and some minor damage in lawns, golf courses, and gardens, in general moles are more beneficial than harmful: their food consists entirely of worms and insects, and they do much to open up the hard-packed subsoil so that it may absorb air and water.

A Robin (*Turdus migratorius*) is a Robin is a Robin. Or is it? According to accurate classification the American Robin is in fact a Thrush. The true Robin is a smaller bird found in Europe.

STAR-NOSED MOLE

OSPREY

BALD EAGLE

AN ACT OF PIRACY

The value of a scavenger like the Bald Eagle (*Haliaeetus leucocephalus*) in the nature of things cannot be over-emphasized. Scavengers are nature's garbage collectors. Without them the earth would become a breeding ground for disease and plague would run rampant.

The Bald Eagle is both a scavenger and a predator; sometimes it will eat small mammals, mainly rodents. It will catch a crippled duck when it can but ninety per cent of its food is fish, usually dead fish, which it finds washed up on the shore.

TALON

Occasionally the Bald Eagle has a taste for fresh fish. However, it is a poor fisherman: any live fish that it can manage to capture are usually spawned-out salmon which require no real fishing ability at all. Occasionally its desire for fresh fish will lead it to harass an air-borne Osprey (*Pandion haliaetus*) that is carrying a fish, forcing the far more skilful fish-catching bird to drop its catch. As the fish falls from the clutches of the Osprey, the eagle swoops down under it and retrieves it before it hits the water.

It was this trait of piracy in the bird's makeup that caused Benjamin Franklin to oppose the choice of the Bald Eagle for the national emblem of the United States: "I wish the bald eagle had not been chosen for the representative of our country.…For in Truth, the turkey is in comparison a much more respectable bird…a bird of courage." ❧

66 Some people say the animals see the straight path and flee from it in fear, for they know that it was built by men. 99

James Houston

very doubtful that it could lift more than its own weight. It is most unlikely, therefore, that the eagle would kill a creature too large for it to carry away. The eagle can kill hares which weigh up to eight pounds (3.6 kg) but does not usually do so. The normal prey of the eagle are mountain hares of six pounds (2.7 kg) or less.

There is some confusion concerning the longevity of eagles. The Golden Eagle is without doubt a long-lived bird: it is believed to be at least four years old before it reaches breeding maturity. A Golden Eagle shot in France in 1845 had a collar around its neck with the date 1750 inscribed on it. If the date on the collar of what was presumably an escaped specimen was the year of its capture then it would appear that this eagle was 95 years old. It is generally conceded that, under optimum conditions in the wild, the Golden Eagle has a lifespan of from 40 to 50 years. ⌁

THE BIRD OF JOVE

Of all the birds of the air it is the Golden Eagle (*Aquila chrysaetos*) which has most inspired the human imagination. The Golden Eagle appears in myths and legends the world over and has been adopted as the emblem of intransigent majesty by emperors and kings throughout history. The Roman legions carried the eagle on their standards in the form of silver and golden ensigns. To the Romans the Golden Eagle belonged to Jupiter or Jove. To Shakespeare, it was the "Bird of Jove".

Contrary to general belief, Golden Eagles do not nest on mountain tops. Many aeries are built on crags only a few hundred feet above sea level. A new nest is generally quite small and may be easily overlooked. However, each year the bird will add to the nest until it becomes a truly monumental structure.

The staple diet of the Golden Eagle consists largely of rabbits, hares, and large game birds. Very occasionally, an eagle develops lamb-killing propensities but this is the exception rather than the rule and generally occurs in areas where the eagle's natural prey is scarce. Eagles are, however, attracted to carrion; the sight of an eagle feeding on a lamb should not be taken to mean that the eagle necessarily had a part in the killing of it.

The size of an animal that the Golden Eagle is capable of killing is often exaggerated. A large eagle weighs ten to twelve pounds (4.5 to 5.4 kg) and it is

WARBLERS

AUGUST

A MALIGNED ANIMAL

Traditionally, wolves have been held in ill repute, and attitudes towards them have been mainly negative. Early settlers feared for their lives because they were often in close proximity to these animals as they worked the small farms they hacked out of heavily wooded areas. The lonely, mournful howl of the wolf was sufficient to instill fear into even the most stout-hearted pioneer.

Recently attitudes have begun to change as people realize that wolves are not a threat to their personal safety, and only rarely to their livestock. There is no authenticated case of a Timber Wolf (*Canis lupus*) ever seriously harming a human in Canada, or on the entire continent for that matter. The fact that workers who trap and tag live wolves find it unnecessary to drug the animals during tagging operations, and never carry firearms, even though they frequently come in contact with the animals, demonstrates that they are not savage. One attack on a human by a rabid wolf has been reported, but the incidence of rabies among wolves is extremely low.

Today, people realize that wolves have positive values and should remain an integral part of our fauna in large parks and wilderness areas. In Ontario's Algonquin Provincial Park, wolves serve as a major tourist attraction; many people travel hundreds of miles in the hope of hearing or seeing a wolf.

The Interpretive Centre at Algonquin Park conducts regular wolf-howling excursions in the park during the month of August. Tape-recorded wolf howls, or human imitations of wolf howls, are used to elicit responses from wild wolves. This participation is most popular and interest is continuing to grow as more people take the opportunity to listen to wild wolves. ∾

CALENDAR

1

Sugaring for **Catocala Moths** can commence. **Zebra Swallowtail Butterfly** (*Graphium marcellus*) captured in Toronto, Ontario, 1943.

8

Largest **North American Lake Trout** (*Salvelinus namaycush*) caught in Lake Athabasca, Saskatchewan (49.5 inches/126 cm, 102 lbs./46 kg), 1961.

10

Smallest known reptile, a species of **Gecko,** was discovered on the island of Virgin Gorda in the Virgin Islands, 1964.

14

Ernest Thompson Seton, Canadian naturalist, born, 1860.

19

A **Pygmy Opossum** (*Eudromicia sp.*), world's rarest mammal, found in a ski hut on Mount Hotham, Victoria, Australia, 1966.

20

Bison (*Bison bison*) first sighted by a European (Henry Kelsey) in Manitoba, 1691.

23

Nighthawks (*Chordeiles minor*) commence annual migration.

24

Regal Fritillary Butterfly (*Speyeria idalia*) captured in Kitchener, Ontario, 1952.

26

Timber Rattlesnake (*Crotalus horridus*) last reported in Canada (Niagara Gorge, Ontario), 1941.

28

Harcourt's Storm Petrel (*Oceanodroma castro*) reported for Canada (Rideau River, Ontario), 1933. **Sooty Tern** (*Sterna fuscata*) reported for Canada (dead specimen near Wolfville, N.S.), 1924. Roger Tory Peterson born, 1908.

29

Last **Eskimo Curlew** (*Numenius borealis*) sighting for Canada (Battle Harbour, Labrador), 1932.

POPULATION EXPLOSION

The numbers of nearly all animals vary over a period of time, responding to favourable weather and many other things, but some kinds are outstanding for their violent fluctuations between scarcity and abundance. Among these the members of the rabbit family are often cited.

There is no simple explanation why excessive population build-ups occur. They are most noticeable among herbivores like rabbits, deer, and mice, whose main purpose is to produce food for flesh-eaters such as hawks, owls, weasels, and foxes. We can imagine that evolutionary processes might have established long ago a system whereby plant-eaters multiplied at a vast rate in order to keep pace with the heavy demand on their numbers, but here nature seems to have gone to extremes.

A surplus of prey species is often far greater than can be taken care of by predators; eventually, however, starvation and disease will result and bring the population numbers back to normal. In the case of deer, starvation caused by over-foraging of the winter food supply is likely to be the deciding factor, but with rabbits, studies have shown that various diseases spreading quickly under crowded conditions drastically reduce the population almost overnight. ∾

COYOTE

Of the 24 species (38 subspecies) of snakes native to Canada, only three (all rattlesnakes) are dangerous to man. The rest are perfectly harmless.

The dangerous varieties are the Northern Pacific Rattlesnake (*Crotalus viridis oreganus*), the Prairie Rattlesnake (*C. v. viridis*), and the Eastern Massasauga Rattlesnake (*Sistrurus catenatus catenatus*). The Timber Rattlesnake (*Crotalus horridus horridus*) was formerly common in the region of Ontario's Niagara Gorge, but since the last positively identified specimen was captured there on August 26, 1941, it is more than likely that this species has been extirpated from Canada. A race of this rattlesnake is still found in parts of the eastern United States where it is known as the Canebrake Rattlesnake (*C.h. atricaudatus*).

Rattlesnakes can be distinguished from non-venomous snakes by the following features: they all possess stout bodies with triangular-shaped heads, and skin patterns that are characteristically

RATTLESNAKE

blotched with black or dark brown on a pale background. The pupils of the eyes of rattlesnakes (as of all venomous snakes) are vertically elliptical like a cat's in the light, while those of non-venomous snakes are round. But perhaps the most characteristic distinguishing feature is the series of bony plates or rattles at the end of the tail, which is exclusive to rattlesnakes.

The species most often encountered in Canada is probably the Eastern Massasauga Rattlesnake. Yet this animal is

rare and endangered, due in no small part to the kill-on-sight attitude held by a large number of people. This snake is restricted to the swamps and bogs around Ontario's Lake Huron and Georgian Bay, and along the north shore of Lake Erie. It is officially recognized as an Ontario Endangered Species, and anyone convicted of molesting or killing a specimen may be liable for a fine of $3,000, six months in jail, or both.

The Massasauga Rattlesnake is mild-mannered and sluggish, seldom exceeds two feet (61 cm) in length, and very rarely attacks humans without provocation. In fact, there are only two records of human fatalities from the bite of this snake. In both cases the snake was handled. Except in areas where children or pets are present LEAVE ALL RATTLESNAKES ALONE! They will then most certainly leave you alone.

If you should have the rare misfortune to be bitten by a rattlesnake, keep all physical activity to an absolute minimum; medical attention should be sought immediately.

Canadian Antivenin Depots are to be found in all areas where rattlesnakes are known to reside:

ONTARIO

Barrie — Royal Victoria Hospital
Bracebridge — Memorial Hospital
Chatham — Public General Hospital
Collingwood — General & Marine
　　Hospital
Espanola — General Hospital
Goderich — Alexandra Marine &
　　General Hospital
Hamilton — General Hospital
Kincardine — General Hospital
Lion's Head — Red Cross Hospital
Little Current — St. Joseph's General
　　Hospital
London — Victoria General Hospital
Meaford — General Hospital
Midland — St. Andrew's Hospital
Orillia — Soldiers' Memorial Hospital
Owen Sound — General & Marine
　　Hospital
Penetanguishene — General Hospital
Parry Sound — General Hospital
　　　　　　 — St. Joseph's General
　　　　　　　　Hospital
Port Colborne — General Hospital
St. Thomas — St. Thomas–Elgin
　　General Hospital
Sarnia — General Hospital
Southampton — Saugeen Memorial
　　Hospital

Sudbury — District Health Unit
Toronto — Provincial Laboratory,
　　Christie Street
　　　　 — Hospital for Sick Children
Welland — County General Hospital
Wiarton — Bruce Peninsula & Dist.
　　Memorial Hospital
Windsor — City Health Department

SASKATCHEWAN

Regina — Provincial Laboratories, Department of Health of Saskatchewan

ALBERTA

Edmonton — Provincial Laboratory of
　　Public Health
Lethbridge — City of Lethbridge
　　Health Unit
Medicine Hat — Medicine Hat
　　Health Unit

BRITISH COLUMBIA

Ashcroft — Ashcroft Hospital
Kamloops — South Central Health Unit
　　& Royal Inland Hospital
Kelowna — Kelowna Hospital
Lytton — Lytton Hospital
Merritt — Merritt Hospital
Oliver — Health Unit Office
Spences Bridge — R.C.M.P.
　　Headquarters
Vernon — Vernon Jubilee Hospital &
　　Vernon Health Unit ❧

FIRST-AID FOR RATTLESNAKE BITES

If medical attention is not immediately available, as may be the case when there is distance to be travelled, then first-aid should be applied. The victim must be kept cool and quiet; undue activity will increase the circulation, allowing the venom to spread more rapidly. If the delay in receiving treatment is going to be lengthy, then a snake-bite kit will be invaluable. The kit consists of a tourniquet, suction devices, an inciser instrument, and an antiseptic.

The suction device should be applied directly to the fang punctures and as much venom withdrawn as possible. This method is considered far preferable to sucking the venom out by using the mouth, as it eliminates the possibility of the toxic substance entering the system by way of a cut lip or gum. Incision should only be applied when there is a considerable delay in receiving treatment, and the instructions provided in the snake-bite kit must be strictly adhered to. In any event, the victim must still be taken to a hospital or a doctor, as the lack of proper treatment of a rattlesnake bite can prove fatal. ❧

The Pronghorn Antelope (*Antilo-capra americana*) of our western plains has a remarkable warning system: it possesses a rump-patch of long, pure-white hair. When danger threatens, the Pronghorn expands this patch into a wide disc and, by widening and narrowing the patch rapidly, it sends out warning flashes, like a ship-to-shore blinker, which can be seen at great distances.

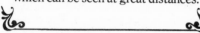 THE HAM ACTOR

The Eastern Hognose Snake (*Hetero-don platyrhinos*) is an extremely rare species that occurs in Canada only in parts of southern Ontario as far north as Parry Sound and the Haliburton region. Because it bears a strong superficial resemblance to a rattlesnake it has been greatly maligned and persecuted within this limited range.

Some people believe that this species has a poisonous breath, toxic enough to cause illness or death to man or beast. Incredibly, you can still find people in farming communities who will assure you that the death of a cow, for example, was caused by this snake's having breathed on it. This sort of myth has undoubtedly been the cause of much unnecessary killing of the Eastern Hognose Snake, thus contributing to its rarity.

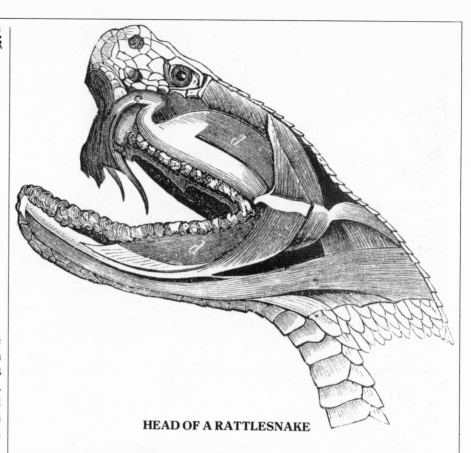

HEAD OF A RATTLESNAKE

In actual fact, this species is one of the most harmless and docile of snakes and feeds almost exclusively on toads and frogs. If disturbed or cornered, however, it goes into a characteristic bluff routine.

When molested it hisses, spreads out its hood in the manner of a cobra, and strikes as though to appear dangerous — yet it never bites. Should this perform-ance fail to intimidate, it will change its tactics dramatically. It goes into convul-sions, writhing in agony, its mouth wide open with its tongue lolling out. Eventu-ally, it rolls on its back and simulates death. When the danger is passed and the snake feels the way to be clear, it will turn itself right way up and make a quick getaway. ∾

RATTLE OF A RATTLESNAKE

RATTLESNAKES

LINNETS

HARE OR RABBIT?

The Varying Hare or Snowshoe Rabbit (*Lepus americanus*) is classed as a hare, although if you follow local usage you will call it a rabbit. The European Hare (*Lepus capensis*), introduced into this country in 1912, is known to everyone as a Jackrabbit, and the most typical North American hares, inhabiting the western part of the continent, are also known as Jackrabbits.

It may seem odd to refer to the same animal as a hare and as a rabbit, but there is no really clearcut difference between the two.

A typical hare has long legs and ears and does not use a den or burrow, but depends on speed to escape from its enemies. Its young are born in an uncovered nest with their eyes open and are able to look after themselves within a few days.

A typical rabbit has shorter ears and legs, uses brushpiles, hollow logs, and burrows for concealment, and its young are born blind and helpless in a hidden nest. In between these two extremes there are many animals not quite typical of either. ~

MOST MODERN BIRDS

The sparrow family is the largest bird family in the world. Of its more than 600 species, 56 have been recorded in Canada.

Sparrows stand high among the songbirds, and they are considered by ornithologists to be the furthest removed of any birds from their primitive ances-

tors. Although many of these birds are coloured in drab browns and greys, this is greatly compensated for by such exceptions as the Rose-breasted Grosbeak (*Pheucticus ludovicianus*), Purple Finch (*Carpodacus purpureus*), Indigo Bunting (*Passerina cyanea*), Evening Grosbeak (*Coccothraustes vespertina*), and American Goldfinch (*Carduelis tristis*), dressed in combinations of black, white, red, yellow, and blue.

In addition to their decorative and musical contributions, these birds are among the most useful to man in his never-ending war against weeds and insects. Many birds destroy insects but eat nothing else, while sparrows eat both insects and weed seeds. This enables them to survive in colder climates than can be tolerated by entirely insectivorous birds, and gives us our attractive assortment of "winter finches".

Whether we call them sparrows, finches, buntings, grosbeaks, or longspurs, they are one of the most fascinating groups of birds, and of great value to mankind. ~

AMERICAN GOLDFINCH

HARE

SEVEN-SPOT LADYBIRDS

Nine-tenths of the world's animals are insects, and outnumber man by more than 300,000 to one. This is a fact which no one who has been in the north woods at the time of year when blackflies, sandflies, and mosquitoes are enjoying their brief, blood-thirsty heyday will dispute. But numerous as these three pests are, they comprise an infinitesimal fraction of the insects that are estimated to exist — in all some 10,000,000 varieties, of which fewer than one-tenth have been classified.

Countless more insects are microscopic than are visible to the naked eye or through a magnifying glass. In the woods, they abound and are so numerous that in one square foot (9.3 dm²) of forest soil, it has been calculated, there is more insect life than there are humans in the world.

Each of these little creatures has a job to do, a purpose to serve, and a relationship to maintain, both with its own kind and with all other living creatures, including man. The relationship cannot be disturbed without upsetting in some way the delicate balance of nature. ∾

PAPER HOUSES

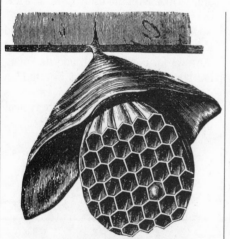

HANGING HORNET'S NEST

The White-faced Hornet (*Vespa sp.*) belongs to a group of insects known as "paper wasps", because they make their own paper for the construction of their houses, or nests. This in itself makes them worthy of a second look, for they are among the few animals that manufacture building material from some quite different substance, in this case, wood. The wood is scraped from the surface of dry and weathered timber — old rail fences are a favourite source of supply — then chewed into a paste with the help of the hornet's paper-making saliva, and shaped to form the nest walls; the paste dries as it is exposed to the air into a tough, grey paper.

When the nest is complete the walls consist of four or five thicknesses of paper each separated from the next by an air space of about ¼ inch (6 mm), provid-

HORNET

ing excellent air circulation and insulation during the hot summer. Inside the inner wall there are three or four circular tiers of cells. One tier may contain more than 400 cells, and a three-tiered nest has a possible production of 1,000 hornets per summer. However, only a mere handful will be alive after the first frosts of September. ∾

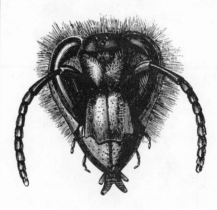

HEAD OF A HORNET

FASTEST LAND ANIMAL

While the Cheetah (*Acinonyx jubatus*) is generally regarded as the fastest mammal on earth over a short distance (i.e., up to 600 yards or 549 m), the title of fastest of all land animals over a sustained distance goes to the Pronghorn (*Antilocapra americana*). It is only when it is hard pressed, however, that the Pronghorn shows evidence of really high speeds.

According to A.S. Einarsen, "On August 14, 1939, I was with a group that paced many Pronghorns on the dried bed of Spanish Lake, in Lake County, Oregon. This lake-bed was as hard as adobe. It was a clear breezy day, ideal to stir the racing instincts of the Pronghorns, and as we rolled along the lake edge we had many challenges. Small groups here and there raced beside the car, until five, led by a magnificent buck, ran parallel to us, pressing towards the shore from the feeding area in the lake centre while we drove on a straight course. As they closed in from the right the buck took a lead of about 50 feet (15 m) and Meyers (Field Observer of the Research Unit at the School of Agriculture, Oregon State College) increased speed to keep even with the animal. Dean Schoenfeld (also of the School of Agriculture) watched the speedometer, Meyers drove the car, and I photographed the moving animals.

"The buck was now about 20 feet (6 m) away and kept abreast of the car at 50 miles an hour (80 km/h). He gradually increased his gait, and with a tremendous burst of speed flattened out so that he appeared as lean and low as a greyhound. Then he turned toward us at about a 45-degree angle and disappeared in front of the car, to reappear on our left. He had gained enough speed to cross our course as the speedometer registered 61 m.p.h. (98 km/h). After the buck had passed us he quickly slackened his pace, and when he reached a rounded knoll about 600 feet (183 m) away he stood snorting, in graceful silhouette, against the sky as though enjoying the satisfaction of beating us in a fair race. No sprinter could have posed in victory with a greater show of gratification. His action was typical and indicated no fright, or he would have continued to run until out of sight."

Assuming that the car speedometer

PRONGHORN

was correct, then this particular Pronghorn must have been travelling at a speed of about 65 miles per hour (105 km/h) as it crossed in front of the car. On other occasions pronghorns have been clocked at 55 miles per hour (89 km/h) over a distance of half a mile (0.8 km).

The Pronghorn has the added distinction of being the only truly native North American ungulate. Other species such as the Moose (*Alces alces*), White-tailed Deer (*Odocoileus virginianus*), and Caribou (*Rangifer tarandus*) all migrated to this continent from Asia via the Bering land bridge during the latter part of the Pleistocene Era, some 10,000 or so years ago. ᨒ

CHEETAH

CECROPIA MOTH

The Monarch Butterfly (*Danaus plexippus*) is the only North American insect proven to exhibit true migrational behaviour.

A number of other insect species occur in Canada as summer immigrants from the south, and a few butterfly species have been observed flying southward in the fall. But whether or not they can be termed truly migrational has yet to be determined. The term "migration" in its strictest sense denotes fairly continuous movement from one area to another with periodic return to the original area. However, in the case of insect migration, it is most frequently taken to mean one-way movement from one area to another with no return flight.

Monarchs can be observed migrating through Ontario's Point Pelee National Park in the fall, some years in such abundance as to form clusters on trees and shrubs. On September 15, 1935 — a particularly good year — Monarchs were observed leaving the Point at the rate of 43 per minute.

The range of the butterfly corresponds

BUTTERFLY MIGRANT

to that of the milkweed, which is the insect's food plant, and both can be seen over most of North America. Seasonally, though, these butterflies are more numerous in certain areas, as they spend the summer months and breed in the northern United States and southern

Canada and migrate south in the late fall. Each spring and fall there is a movement of Monarchs from one range to the other.

During their flight the Monarchs reach speeds of thirty miles per hour (48 km/h). The longest recorded flight is more than 1,800 miles (2,897 km) from Ontario to the Sierra Madre Mountains, their wintering ground in central Mexico. The fall migration is, of course, more spectacular, augmented as it is by a new generation of Monarchs moving south. This phenomenon may be observed at Point Pelee each year in late September and early October. Great numbers enter the park and gather on trees at the very tip of the Point before they cross Lake Erie. Their numbers build to a peak every five to seven years when the population reaches enormous proportions.

Perhaps the most baffling aspect of this migration is the fact that every year a new crop of butterflies undertakes this trip with no aid or direction from the previous generation. Their elders have died out by departure time. ᥄

6

First **Carolina Wren** (*Thryrothorus ludovicianus*) sighting in Canada (Point Pelee, Ontario), 1905. Heaviest horse ever recorded, "Brooklyn Supreme", died in Callender, Iowa (3,200 lbs./1,451 kg), 1948.

7

Anhinga (*Anhinga anhinga*) reported for Canada (Wellington, Ontario), 1904.

11

Scarlet Ibis (*Gouara rubra*) (possible escapee) first observed in Canada (Point Pelee, Ontario), 1941.

CALENDAR

15

Monarch Butterflies (*Danaus plexippus*) observed migrating at a rate of 43 per minute (Point Pelee, Ontario), 1935. **Bottle-nosed Dolphin** (*Tursiops truncatus*) in Canadian waters (Petitcodiac River, N.B.), 1950.

16

70,000 **Broad-winged Hawks** (*Buteo platypterus*) seen at Hawk Cliff, Ontario, 1961.

22

First **Northern Fur Seal** (*Callorhinus sp.*) reported for Canada (Queen Charlotte Strait, B.C.), 1944.

25

Yellow-breasted Chat (*Icteria virens*) in northern Ontario (Caribou Island, Thunder Bay), 1979. A **Silver-haired Bat** (*Lasionycteris noctivagans*) found among flocks of birds at Long Point Lighthouse, Ontario, 1929.

26

Pipevine Swallowtail Butterfly (*Battus philenor*) sighted in northern Ontario (Caribou Island), 1979.

METAMORPHOSIS OF THE LUNA MOTH

SILK MOTHS

When you are crunching through the leaves during the fall, watch carefully for the cocoons of moths.

Among the moths found in Canada, the Silk Moths are the largest and the most attractive. The most familiar and widely ranging species are the Cecropia (*Hyalophora cecropia*), Polyphemus (*Antheraea polyphemus*), and Luna (*Actias luna*).

The main characteristics of Silk Moths are their large expansive wings marked with eye-spots, which are transparent in some cases. Their bodies are stout and furry, and in most cases are as brightly coloured as their wings. The antennae or feelers are strongly feathered in the males, much less so in the females. With a few exceptions, Silk Moths fly at night and are strongly attracted to light.

The caterpillars are large and stout, usually green and often ornamented with brightly coloured spines called tubercles.

Winter is spent as pupae in long or oval cocoons made of silk. From late fall until spring they can readily be seen as they hang from leafless trees or lie among the fallen leaves.

The very handsome Cecropia is the largest of all our native moths; a large female may reach a span of almost seven inches (18 cm). It is common throughout most of Canada east of the Rocky Mountains. The colour of the wings is grey, tinged with red in a wavy white line extending across both wings along the margin. There is a transparent eye-spot on each wing. The body is bright red, banded with white. The female lays between two hundred and three hundred oval white eggs on the underside of the leaves of its food tree in late spring and early summer.

When fully mature, the caterpillar that hatches from the egg is about four inches (10 cm) long, green, and decorated with blue, yellow, and red tubercles. It feeds on the leaves of various trees, especially cherry, plum, apple, willow, maple, birch, and elderberry.

The cocoon spun by the caterpillar is the largest of any moth and varies in colour, though usually a smoky grey, and is attached vertically to a twig. West of the Rocky Mountains, the Cecropia is replaced by a very closely related species, Glover's Silk Moth (*Hyalophora gloveri*), which is almost identical in its markings to the Cecropia except that its ground colour is a beautiful port wine, and it is a little smaller.

The Polyphemus is the most common of our Silk Moths, ranging throughout southern Canada from coast to coast. It is named after the one-eyed Cyclops in Homer's *Odyssey* because of the large eye-spot on its hindwing. Only a little smaller than the Cecropia, a large specimen will measure 5½ to 6 inches (14 to 15 cm). It is variable in colour, ranging from a pale cream to a rich terracotta. Usually it is a delicate shade of tawny yellow with a large blue and yellow eye-spot on the hindwing. On the forewing there is a smaller transparent spot. In Canada, there is only one brood a year, while farther south there are two. The moth is active generally about the first week in June and flys throughout the month into July. The female lays bun-shaped eggs individually or in clusters.

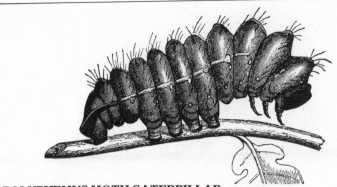

POLYPHEMUS MOTH CATERPILLAR

The caterpillar is accordion-shaped, large and green, often with a bluish tinge, with red tubercles. It feeds on a wide range of food trees including oak, hickory, elm, maple, and birch. The cocoon is oval, tough, and parchment-like; it is attached to a twig rolled up in a leaf. When the leaf dies and falls to the ground, the cocoon falls with it, and spends the winter there among the leaves. It was once thought that the silk produced by the Polyphemus could be used for commercial purposes, but the weave proved to be non-continuous and therefore unsatisfactory.

The Luna is the most beautiful of all North American insects. It is noted for its delicate green colouring and exquisite wing symmetry. The green very rapidly fades to a yellowish grey when exposed to direct sunlight for any length of time. Its body is white-furred, its eye-spots small and transparent and surrounded with rings of pale yellow, blue, and black. The forewings have a purplish outer margin. A large Luna will measure $4^3/_4$ inches (12 cm) across its wings.

It is seen less often than the two preceding species because it prefers thickly wooded areas. It is found in most of southern Canada east of the Rocky Mountains. When flying at night, the Luna's unusual shape and floating flight give it an eerie, ghost-like appearance.

HUMMINGBIRD SPHINX MOTH

The eggs are a shiny bluish-green and are laid individually or in clusters on the host plant, which may be walnut, chestnut, pecan, birch and possibly willow, gum, persimmon, and others of the ebony family. The cocoon is thin and compact and is usually spun among leaves on the ground. ∽

OUR TINIEST NATIVE HAWK

The American Kestrel (*Falco sparverius*) is especially renowned for its ability to hover low over fields, appearing almost motionless except for the fast beating of its wings, while seeking out its prey. During this activity, its hovering and slender pointed wings provide good identification marks.

Despite its former name of "Sparrow Hawk", insects such as grasshoppers, crickets, beetles, and caterpillars are the mainstay of its diet. It also favours mice and lizards.

Between nine and twelve inches (23 and 30 cm) in length, it is the smallest, commonest, and probably the most beautiful of our native hawks. The female is generally larger and differently coloured. The adult male has a blue-grey head, nape, and wing coverts, with only the crown and tail a rufous red. The adult female is extensively reddish-brown, including the tail, which is relatively unbarred. Both sexes have the handsome black and white face pattern, and both birds utter the high-pitched repetitive call note "killy, killy, killy".

This is the small raptor that is often seen on telegraph poles, sitting somewhat erect, with occasional jerkings of its tail. It nests generally in a tree cavity, usually one that has been previously bored by a flicker. In rural areas it nests in niches in barns and towers, and there are generally four to seven creamy-white eggs heavily blotched with various shades of rich cinnamon brown. The American Kestrel's breeding range extends from Alaska to Nova Scotia, and south to the West Indies and South America. It overwinters from southern Canada southward. ∽

AMERICAN KESTREL

71

THE EDGE OF EXTINCTION

An estimated 60 million Bison (*Bison bison*), commonly called "buffalo", roamed much of the North American continent before the coming of the European settlers. They undoubtedly formed the greatest large-mammal congregations that ever existed on earth. Huge bison herds moved like a black sea across the plains, covering them for miles around.

WOOD BISON

When the Europeans began their westward drive over the plains of North America, the bison were slaughtered at an alarming rate. However, an estimated 40 million bison still survived in the West as late as 1830 and it was not until the construction of the Central Pacific and Union Pacific railroads in 1869 that the herds began to be annihilated.

The animals' last days began in the 1870s but even then they seemed to march without end. Near Fort Hays, Kansas, in September 1871, a troop of the Sixth Cavalry came upon a herd that numbered in the hundreds of thousands. "For six days," reported the young commander, "we continued our way through this enormous herd, during the last three of which it was in constant motion across our path." He found it impossible to "approximate the millions".

Some of the killing was for meat and hides but much of it was for sport. In many instances, even when the bison were killed for food, only the tongue was saved. It is estimated that ignorance of the methods of curing hides resulted in the saving of only one out of every three or four hides.

In the late 1800s, professional bison hunters, such as William F. Cody, better known as "Buffalo Bill", were hired to supply food for the crews working on the

BISON

railroads: "I killed buffalo for the railroad company for twelve months, and during that time the number I brought into camp was kept account of and at the end of that period I had killed 4,280 buffalo." Between 1872 and 1874 well over a million animals were shot yearly. No animal population could withstand such an onslaught.

The Plains Bison (*Bison bison bison*) might have disappeared from Canada had not an Indian named Walking Coyote saved four bison calves from slaughter in 1873, during a hunting expedition along the Milk River in northwestern Montana. Also, a Winnipeg fur dealer saved another five calves a year later. Walking Coyote drove his calves into Montana where, by 1914, their descendents numbered 745. In that year those 745 bison and the 87 offspring of the calves saved in Winnipeg were released in Wood Buffalo National Park in the Northwest Territories. By 1954, the offspring of the original nine calves numbered 40,000, making the comeback of the Plains Bison one of Canada's great conservation victories.

AMERICAN BISON

THE HORROR OF TRAPPING IN CANADA

Over the years untold numbers of fur-bearing mammals have been, and continue to be, slaughtered for their fur in the cruellest and most painful manner possible.

Although Canada was originally founded on its trapping industry, many Canadians may not be aware of some of the methods used in the capturing of these animals and the extent of their misery. The main source of suffering is imposed by the leg-hold or steel-jaw trap.

First invented in Great Britain, it was subsequently brought to Canada around the early part of the last century. It was an abomination, as barbaric and cruel a means of torture as could possibly be conceived. But in its day it was the only known effective device for capturing wild animals for the fur trade, and so it had a very valid purpose. However, with the radically changing times, it should long ago have been discarded along with the rack and the thumb-screw.

An animal caught in a leg-hold trap suffers excruciating pain and terror, eventually dying of starvation or exposure after several days. The desperation of an animal caught in this way often causes it to gnaw off its paws in a frantic effort to escape. It is quite a common occurrence for an animal to escape with its severed foot still in the trap. This is known to trappers as a "wring off", and is a complete waste. Apart from the suffering caused to the animal, the trapper has lost his pelt. Any animal thus hampered by a missing paw or two is highly vulnerable to gangrene and is totally unable to defend itself against its enemies, or to pursue its prey. A painful and inevitable death is all it can look forward to.

Many trappers openly deplore the cruelty of the leg-hold trap, and there are many quotations to support this from trappers across the country. One writes: "I once saw a large beaver caught by the front leg. The flesh was entirely gone to the bare white bone, and in its struggles to escape from my approach the bone snapped with a sickening crack."

A one-time trapper describes a scene after finding a domestic cat accidentally caught in a leg-hold trap set for a bobcat: "One look was enough to tell us how

ARCTIC FOXES IN WINTER DRESS

terribly the cat had suffered before death set it free from its agony. The bark was torn from the trees and even the earth was torn up. A look of terrible pain was frozen on the animal's features.... Since that time we have never set a steel trap."

A radio network supervisor writes: "Years ago as a small boy on the prairies, I set out my first tiny trapline. Returning the next day I found a rabbit in my first trap, its leg shattered and broken bone exposed. It was still alive and crying like a baby. I pulled my trapline and never set another."

Over 75 per cent of the animals trapped in Canada fall into the category of "semi-aquatic" (beaver, muskrat, mink, and otter) and a great percentage of these are trapped either in or near water. This method is supposed to be more humane as the animal drowns while being trapped, thereby shortening its period of suffering. However, it is debatable whether it is in fact more humane; a beaver, for example, may take up to twenty minutes to die under such conditions, and the fear and panic incurred during drowning may in fact be intensified.

Many animals that are taken in leg-hold traps, moreover, are taken by accident and have absolutely no commercial value. The leg-hold trap is completely

unselective. Some of these victims include birds, such as ducks, Blue and Grey Jays, eagles, owls, and mammals, such as snowshoe hares, flying squirrels, and porcupines. A five-year survey conducted by the Ontario Ministry of Natural Resources states that on two traplines, using only leg-hold traps, 1,350 unwanted birds and mammals were caught.

Snares have also been used in some areas. These are simply strong wires formed into a loop that will tighten around the animal's neck and strangle it. Here again, this trapping method is supposed to be more humane, and it undoubtedly can be so. But a snare has to be set with the greatest of care by a professional or instead of catching the animal around the neck, the loop may tighten around the animal's middle. Apparently, there have been many such mishaps involving rabbits. The result is that the blood circulation in the animal is completely cut off, and in frigid weather the rear half of the animal freezes solid, while the front part is still alive. Even if a snare is set correctly an animal can still take fifteen minutes or longer to die by strangulation.

To give an idea of the number of our fur-bearing animals that are trapped and snared each year, the remaining 20 to 25 per cent of "non-aquatic" animals taken in Ontario alone represents well over 100,000 specimens. This is just a small amount of the suffering that is carried on right across Canada each year, suffering that many people do not know about or prefer not to dwell on.

Substantial efforts have been made, however, within the last decade to create more humane methods of trapping in this country. This has entailed the search for alternative traps, and the advent of trapper-education courses, such as those currently being conducted in Ontario.

In many parts of Canada, the leg-hold trap has been supplanted by the Conibear trap, which is generally considered to be far less brutal if set correctly and applied only to non-aquatic animals. The effect of the Conibear trap on aquatic species, however, is not fully understood, due in no small part to the difference in the physiology of these animals. More field study needs to be conducted on this subject.

The Federal-Provincial Committee for Humane Trapping (FPCHT), a government-sponsored organization, together with the Canadian Association for Humane Trapping (CAHT) are currently conducting research programs into alternative traps for more humane trapping. Here are some of the traps being worked on:

THE GABRY

Invented by Mr. Bill Gabry of British Columbia. This trap has shown itself to be humane for Mink and Marten under controlled situations, and is now being field tested.

THE BIONIC

Another invention of Mr. Gabry. The Bionic Trap has proved itself successful under controlled conditions.

THE CONIBEAR 120

The earlier model, the single-spring Conibear 110, has shown itself to be incapable of killing Mink and Marten consistently, and therefore should not be used for these animals. However, the double-spring Conibear 120 was also inconsistent in the trapping of these animals, when they were hit on the neck, rather than the head or thorax. This trap is currently being upgraded and the modifications look promising.

THE VITAL

Perhaps the most interesting killer-type trap being worked on at present, and as far as is known, is the first trap to be designed to predetermined standards. This trap is being field tested this coming trapping season.

THE ONTARIO LEGSNARE AND THE SWEDISH LEGSNARE

These traps, designed to be more humane alternatives to the leghold, are now being field tested. The trapped animals are held by the leg, by a cable, not by steel jaws. It is hoped that this device will provide a more humane alternative in situations where killing traps are either inadequate or are a danger to domestic animals. One advantage of the Ontario Legsnare is that it will be about the same cost to produce as the leg-hold. The Swedish Legsnare, on the other hand, presently costs about eighty dollars, or fifteen to twenty times more than the leg-hold.

The public is strongly urged to support the endeavours of the Canadian Association for Humane Trapping. Further information may be obtained by writing to: Canadian Association for Humane Trapping, Box 934, Station F, Toronto, Ontario. M4Y 2N9

THE PASSENGER PIGEON

Abundance is no guarantee of survival. The Passenger Pigeon (*Ectopistes migratorius*) was the most abundant of all recorded bird species, and was estimated to have numbered between five and nine billion before 1840, constituting 25 per cent of the total bird population of North America.

These birds moved about in such incredible numbers as to stagger the imagination. One flock of pigeons seen by Major W.R. King in 1866, at Mississauga, Ontario, is the largest flock of birds to have ever been recorded. Major King reported that it took fourteen hours to pass overhead and for several days afterwards, smaller flocks of "weaker or younger birds" continued to fly past. It has been calculated that this flock of birds contained 3,717,120,000 pigeons.

The sudden and complete disappearance of the Passenger Pigeon is probably the most remarkable in all zoological history. Their extinction was brought about by the unlimited killing of these birds, which were a valuable source of food. A dozen pigeons could be bought for less than a dollar at a market in Canada; the breast meat was eaten while the wings and feathers were used to fill potholes in the road. Their habit of nesting in huge colonies made them an easy target for the guns and nets of the thousands of professional hunters who caught them for profit. The destruction of the eastern deciduous forest, which contained their feeding, nesting, and roosting areas, may also have been a major contributing factor.

The last recorded Passenger Pigeons in Canada were a pair observed at Penetanguishene, Ontario, on May 18, 1902, and the species became extinct when the last living specimen, Martha, died in the Cincinnati Zoological Gardens on September 1, 1914.

"They now congregate into immense flocks and I am told that it is no uncommon thing to kill thirty or forty birds at a single discharge from an ordinary fowling piece. Most of the inhabitants that have guns in their possession, now, as well as at other periods when the pigeons make their appearance, turn out and slaughter vast numbers. Pigeons being now the order of the day from one end of

PASSENGER PIGEON

the country to the other. Almost every family is treating themselves with a mess of these birds. It is astonishing what prodigious quantities are killed and yet to all appearances their numbers are not lessened even in the slightest degree. I am told by credible persons that they do not observe any decrease in the vast flocks of these birds but that they appear still as large and as numerous as they did twenty or thirty years back.

"Sometimes for the space of a week or fortnight flocks of pigeons from twenty to one or two hundred in a flock will keep passing over a certain district all in the same direction and one flock appearing as soon as the previous one is lost sight of, following each other in quick succession. At such times a shooter has nothing to do but to place himself in a favourable situation and he may continue firing at each succeeding flock all the live-long day till at last he grows weary with the work of destruction."

William Pope ∽ September 1834

66 It is a fact that for centuries we have lived by *killing* cod and other fish; by *killing* seals in the water and on the ice, and animals on land;...Has all this developed in us a trait of destructiveness, or narcotized what ought naturally to be an instinct for creativeness? 99

J. R. Smallwood

The next time a Skunk (*Mephitis mephitis*) leaves its unmistakeable scent in your neighbourhood, you might take some comfort in knowing that, according to one scientist, the Skunk destroys more insects than all other mammals combined. The Skunk's diet includes grubs, grasshoppers, potato beetles, caterpillars, and crickets.

FIELD VOLE

OCTOBER

BIRDS OF PREY

The value of birds of prey to our entire economy is easily traceable to the depredations of rodents to which we would be subjected were it not for these birds.

The Meadow Mouse (*Microtus pennsylvanicus*), also known as the Field Mouse, Field Vole, or Meadow Vole, and other subspecies merit a word by themselves in any discussion of the habits of our native birds of prey since mice form such a large proportion of their diet, especially the diet of owls. The Meadow Mouse is interesting, not only for this reason but also because it carries the distinction of being the most numer-ous mammal on the North American continent and is one of the most destructive of all nature's forces with which producers of foodstuffs must contend.

Not only do Meadow Mice destroy grass; they feed voraciously on roots, bulbs, tubers, twigs, flowers, seeds, and foliage and they cause great injury by girdling trees, shrubs, and vines. The effects of removing or diminishing the natural enemies of this creature would be devastating. It is ironic, therefore, that the very persons who benefit most from the creatures who prey on this animal are the ones who in turn prey on them. ༄

CALENDAR

2

Sage Sparrow (*Amphispiza belli*) sighted in Canada (Lulu Island, B.C.), 1930. Eastern **Tiger Salamander** (*Ambystoma tigrinum*) recorded for Canada (Point Pelee, Ontario), 1915.

8

Blue-winged Warbler (*Vermivora pinus*) sighted in northern Ontario (Marathon), 1979.

13

Orange-barred Sulphur Butterfly (*Phoebis philea*) sighted in Canada (Vineland, Ontario), 1930.

15

Red-legged Kittiwake (*Rissa brevirostris*) sighted in Canada (dead specimen found near Fortymile, Yukon), 1899. Peak of **Saw-whet Owl** (*Aegolius acadicus*) migration on Toronto Island, Ontario.

19

Largest worm found in Britain (Hauxley Bay, Northumberland), 38 inches (97cm), 1975.

21

Marine Mammal Protection Act passed, 1972.

22

Royal Tongan Tortoise (*Testudo sp.*) reputedly presented to the King of Tonga by Captain Cook. **Golden-winged Warbler** (*Vermivora chrysoptera*) sighted in northern Ontario (Marathon), 1979.

23

Ernest Thompson Seton, Canadian naturalist, died, 1946.

29

Vermillion Flycatcher (*Pyrocephalus rubinus mexicanus*) sighted in Canada (Toronto, Ontario), 1949.

30

Bar-tailed Godwit (*Limosa lapponica*) reported for Canada (Colebrook, B.C.), 1931.

GOSHAWK

THE IMPORTANCE OF PREDATORS

Predators are often the subject of abuse, their way of life is often regarded as cruel, and they are sometimes described as wicked.

Granted that no one can watch a hawk taking chickens with equanimity, it will still be realized that the only and normal way a predator lives is by killing, and that man himself is the greatest killer of all, as witness the daily stockyard reports. We, however, mostly conduct our predation away from public sight, unless, of course, we are hunting. The wild predators lack our resources and must kill by the only means they have, when and where they can. In doing this they are a normal part of the environment and have been so for as long as fossils enable us to read the record.

Quite some time ago, Julian Huxley

CARIBOU

was said to have remarked that to have the right enemies is an asset to a species. Consider the deer–wolf chain as an example. By and large, the deer which are less efficient, whether through age, infirmity, size, or disease, will be taken by wolves, leaving the fitter specimens to carry on the herd. This means that the predator exerts selection and so helps maintain the standard of the population.

There is little difference between a man who can run a hundred yards (91 m) in ten seconds and one who takes fifteen, but if the man were in the place of a hunted deer, it might well decide whether he became a predator's meal or not.

Past events have shown us that when a herd of deer is relieved of predation, it becomes too large for its food supply and readily succumbs to starvation and disease. There are established cases of populations of grouse being nearly wiped out by epidemic disease when their predators have been drastically reduced. Predators are, therefore, a normal and essential element in a balanced and healthy population. ∞

MARSH HAWKS

78

THE MOVE TOWARDS CONSERVATION

The conservation movement in Canada commenced, as in the United States, with the establishment of large national parks, and both countries have worked together almost from the beginning. It was the dawn of the twentieth century, and passing of laws were to follow that would preserve the animals that barely survived the nineteenth century. Our national symbol, the Beaver (*Castor canadensis*), saved when the silk top hat supplanted the fashionable felted beaver hat, was nearly extinct at the turn of the century. The Bison (*Bison bison*) were nearly gone, as were the Pronghorns (*Antilocapra americana*), and a host of other species.

Freebooting market hunting and habitat destruction had brought catastrophe to much of the continent's wildlife. But now there was to be an era of enlightenment, as hunters and fishermen began to band together to get provincial legislators to pass laws setting closed seasons and hunting limits. Subsequently, hunting and fishing licences were introduced to raise funds for paying game wardens to enforce the new game laws. Today, every province has its wildlife agencies whose primary responsibility it is to ensure the welfare of game species.

However, this beneficial attitude towards wildlife which flourished at the time did not apply equally to all species. Paradoxically, a certain element of the fauna fell victim as never before to widespread animosity; these were the predatory animals which were still branded as vermin, even by many professional zoologists. The birds of prey, or raptors, enjoyed an uneasy sanctuary in some parts of their range, but carnivorous mammals were everywhere persecuted under that "tool" of wildlife management known today as predator control.

Banff National Park, authorized in 1885, was the first park of its kind in Canada, and the magnificent Jasper Park was among the four other national parks that had been set up by 1908.

More were to follow. Wood Buffalo National Park was established in 1922 in the Northwest Territories and Alberta originally to preserve the last descendants of the Wood Bison; it also contains the last known breeding grounds of the Whooping Crane (*Grus americana*). Over 10,000 square miles (25,900 km^2) in area, it is several times the size of Yellowstone National Park, the largest park in the United States.

The Waterton National Park and Quetico Forest Reserve adjoin and complement Glacier National in Montana and the Minnesota National Forest, their respective counterparts in the United States, and there are, as well, a number of

ADULT GOSHAWK AND RABBIT

enormous game preserves in the Yukon and Northwest Territories on which hunting and trapping rights are restricted to Inuit and Indians.

Canada had twenty-three national parks in 1971; today there are twenty-eight. Most recently established are the Nahanni National Park, along the South Nahanni River in the Northwest Territories; Auyuittuq National Park on the Cumberland Peninsula of Baffin Island; and Kluane National Park in the Yukon.

Co-operation between Canadian and U. S. conservation groups has been extensive and effective. The treaties protecting the fur seals and the migratory birds were fine early examples, and the Canada breeding grounds of the latter are the joint concern of both nations. The Seal Treaty of 1911 witnessed the first significant federal intervention in the cause of wildlife conservation, while the Migratory Bird Convention Act of 1917 offered protection for birds that regularly cross the borders of the two nations.

By the mid-sixties, however, much of our wildlife was declining so rapidly that naturalists began to talk in desperate terms. The most recent threat to wildlife and the cause of so much of this concern was what has been loosely termed "technological fallout". In the course of our efforts to achieve ever-higher living standards, many new materials have been developed and thrust upon the environment without regard for the consequences. Perhaps the most serious of those recognized were the pesticides.

Dichloro-diphenyl-trichloroethane (DDT) was just the first and best known of the synthetic compounds that seemed the answer to mankind's long war on insect pests. But no one could foresee the far-reaching effects of DDT and the other chlorinated hydrocarbons that were soon to be developed. These chlorinated hydrocarbons came to be known as the "deadly seven": apart from DDT, they include aldrin, chlordane, dieldrin, endrin, lindane, and heptachlor. However, after a while insects developed an immunity to the poisons and the survivors showed a tolerance for two or three times the dose that had killed 99 per cent of previous generations, and they were able to reproduce successfully.

The top predators, especially the fish-eating birds of prey, were found to be most vulnerable to this new chemical hazard because they prey mainly on the unwary, the sick, the dying, and the dead, those most heavily laden with pesticide poisons. Each meal adds immeasurably to the concentration held in their own

BEAVER

WHY DID THE DINOSAURS DISAPPEAR?

Dinosaurs were reptiles that lived and died in the Mesozoic Era, between 75 and 215 million years ago. Remains of these prehistoric animals have been found on every continent, from the Arctic to Patagonia at the tip of South America, and from Great Britain to China.

Although all dinosaurs were reptiles, not all reptiles were dinosaurs. Those which lived in the sea, such as the Ichthyosaurs and Plesiosaurs, and those that glided on naked wings such as the Pterosaurs, were not dinosaurs. Also, dinosaurs varied greatly in size and structure: some were no bigger than a large dog, while others, like the Diplodocus, reached an enormous 85 feet (26 m) in length, and a weight of 30 or more tons (27,216 kg). Yet, despite their impressive sizes, the largest of the dinosaurs (the Diplodocus and Brachiosaurus) pale in comparison with the Blue Whale (*Balaenoptera musculus*) that may attain a length of 100 feet (30 m) and a weight of 150 tons (136,078 kg), and has the distinction of being the largest creature to have ever lived on this earth.

It is generally believed that most dinosaurs must have been fairly harmless, slow-moving creatures that fed entirely on plants. And that they were in turn preyed upon by ferocious, sharp-toothed flesh-eaters that moved around on strong, muscular hind legs with their bodies bent forward and their tails off the ground as a counterbalance.

In Canada, dinosaurs have been found in Alberta and Saskatchewan, fragmentary bones in Nova Scotia, and footprints along the Peace River in British Columbia. Remains have also been found on Bathurst Island in the Northwest Territories.

bodies. Even if they grow to maturity, reproduction suffers in the failure of eggs to develop the usual amount of calcium in the eggshell. The too-thin eggshells are unable to withstand the wear and tear of incubation and the eggs fail to hatch. Consequently, since the almost total ban on the use of DDT in Canada in 1971, many of these populations have shown signs of a slight resurgence.

The largest wildlife organization in Canada is the Canadian Wildlife Federation, founded in 1962, as the result of the Resources for Tomorrow Conference, held in Montreal in 1961. Its efforts are largely aimed at educating Canadians in the importance of natural resources, especially in the necessity of maintaining wildlife species. The Canadian Wildlife Act of 1973 provides a firmer base for co-operative studies to protect and preserve endangered species.

Today, most biologists agree that the major threat to animals is the destruction of their living space through the expansion of man's growing population. With that in mind the Province of Ontario developed the Endangered Species Act of 1973 in order to preserve endangered species and their habitats in Ontario. The Ontario species currently protected by the Endangered Species Act are:

Bald Eagle (*Haliaeetus leucocephalus*); Golden Eagle (*Aquila chrysaetos*); Eastern Peregrine Falcon (*Falco peregrinus anatum*); White Pelican (*Pelecanus erythrorhynchos*); Eskimo Curlew (*Numenius borealis*); Piping Plover (*Charadrius melodus*); Kirtland's Warbler (*Dendroica kirtlandii*); Eastern Cougar (*Felis concolor cougar*); Timber Rattlesnake (*Crotalus-horridus-horridus*); Eastern Massassauga Rattlesnake (*Sistrurus catenatus catenatus*); Blue Racer (*Coluber constrictor foxi*); Lake Erie Water Snake (*Nerodia sipedon insularum*); West Virginia White Butterfly (*Pieris virginiensis*); and the Small White Lady's Slipper (Orchid) (*Cypripedium candidum*). The penalty for molesting or killing a protected species in Ontario is a maximum fine of $3,000, six months in jail, or both.

In mid-1974, New Brunswick passed an Endangered Species Act patterned after Ontario's statute. Regulations were promulgated February 11, 1976, covering five species: Eastern Cougar (*Felis concolor cougar*); Canada Lynx (*Lynx canadensis*); Bald Eagle (*Haliaeetus leucocephalus*); Osprey (*Pandion haliaetus*); and Peregrine Falcon (*Falco peregrinus anatum*).

TRICERATOPS

ICHTHYOSAURUS AND PLESIOSAURUS

The extinction of the dinosaurs is generally regarded as one of the greatest mysteries of the world. And yet, if we were to follow their history we would find that some kinds were disappearing and diversifying throughout all the stages of their development, so that the last of the dinosaurs differed greatly from their own ancestors.

Throughout their long evolution they became increasingly larger, so that more food and space was required to facilitate their great bulk. It is well known that there were also changes in the relationship of land and water throughout the Mesozoic Era, together with the changes in vegetation and the inevitable changes in climate. Each and all of these factors would have had an effect on the dinosaurs.

Under these conditions, food would undoubtedly have become more difficult to acquire for the large vegetarians. Large animals tend to have fewer young and they would, therefore, be at a distinct disadvantage in the increased competition for food. The cooling of the climate towards the latter part of the Mesozoic (the Cretaceous Period, 170 to 136 million years ago) while not affecting the dinosaurs directly if they were warm-blooded (as some experts believe), would certainly have affected the vegetation, and thus added to the difficulties of the many different kinds of dinosaurs.

Compounding this was the gradually increasing competition from other animals. The reptiles, themselves, produced very large crocodiles in the Cretaceous, capable of dealing with large dinosaurs; mammals were also making themselves known. They were mainly small but their predations on dinosaur eggs and young at such a critical time may have hastened the dinosaurs' passing.

So it can be seen that there were many reasons why the dinosaurs should disappear at a time when all the continents were being slowly reshaped. All the dinosaurs had gone by the end of the Cretaceous. ⌦

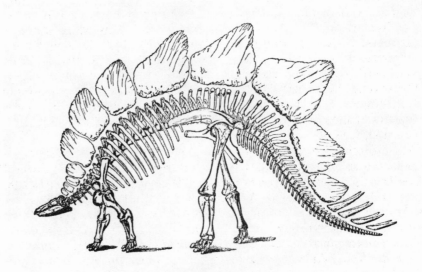

SKELETON OF THE ARMOURED DINOSAUR

summer and provide suitable areas of open water for seals. Where the icepack is constantly moving, causing it to break up even in winter, as is the case off Alaska and the northeastern coast of Greenland, the conditions are peculiarly suited to the requirements of seals. Polar Bears are more common on these coasts than in most parts of the Arctic.

The Polar Bear (*Ursus maritimus*) has its own snow tires. The bottoms of its paws are covered with short, stiff hair which not only keeps its paws warm but also gives it good traction on snow and ice.

TOO FAR NORTH FOR A POLAR BEAR

During the last glaciation period the Polar Bear (*Ursus maritimus*) lived south of its present range. In 1690, a German naturalist named Von Siebold reported that Polar Bears reached the northern island of Japan and that they were once more common in the Bering Strait and in Iceland than they are now.

Most people think of the Polar Bear as having always lived at the North Pole and nowhere else. Actually, the North Pole is too far north for even a Polar Bear to survive. However, individual bears have been seen in the frozen Arctic Ocean as far as 88° latitude north — only two degrees from the North Pole. A most unusual record was that of an old female that was shot near Peribonca, Lake St. John district, in Quebec, on or about October 29, 1938.

The almost total absence of Polar Bears on the Canadian arctic islands is due to the fact that the inshore ice of those coasts does not break up every

SAW-WHET OWLS

Probably the most outstanding feature of birding in Toronto is the large number of Saw-whet Owls (*Aegolius acadicus*) that regularly migrate through that region in the fall. The Toronto Island Bird Sanctuary, between Hanlan's Point and Centre Island, has long been regarded as one of the best sites for these migrating birds in North America. Over 100 specimens are regularly banded here each year.

Starting the first week in October the migration continues to the second week in November, with a peak period around mid-October. As mice constitute the mainstay of the owls' diet, whenever there is a shortage of these animals in their area they are forced to seek food elsewhere. Under normal circumstances, they tend to spend the winter seeking sustenance in favourable locations in the southerly parts of their breeding grounds.

Their breeding range extends from southern Alaska south to Mexico.

Saw-whet Owls spend the daylight hours asleep, or perched motionless and well concealed in willows. At this time they are absurdly tame and easily approached, allowing themselves to be handled without showing any sign of alarm. This trait makes them easy prey for their arch enemy, the Barred Owl (*Strix varia*). They become active with the onset of dusk. In flight their chunky bodies and short, rounded wings are somewhat suggestive of the American Woodcock (*Philohela minor*).

Except for the Pygmy Owl (*Glaucidium gnoma*) of the west, the Saw-whet, which is only seven or eight inches (18 or 20 cm) long, is the smallest of Canadian owls. It varies from fawn-brown to greyish-brown with white spots on its wings. Its underparts are pale and prominently streaked with chestnut-brown. Bright yellow eyes are set in a conspicuous facial disc. The Saw-whet Owl may be readily distinguished from the Screech Owl (*Otus asio*) by its lack of ear-tufts, and from the Boreal Owl (*Aegolius funereus*) by its smaller size and lack of white spots on the crown.

The rather unusual name of Saw-whet Owl is derived from the rasping character of one of its calls which sounds like a large-toothed saw being filed. ⌒

COMMON REDPOLL

mation the figure would also appear to have been high. Most bird kills were recorded after rather sudden drops in temperature following the arrival of cold fronts. On two such occasions Saw-whet Owls (*Aegolius acadicus*) were observed in trees close to the Toronto-Dominion Centre. It was conjectured that they were lying in wait to prey upon the smaller and weaker birds that would come to grief.

Migratory bird casualties ranged from Whip-poor-Wills (*Caprimulgus vociferus*) to a Ruby-throated Hummingbird (*Archilochus colubris*), and prominently featured White-throated Sparrows (*Zonotrichia albicollis*), Common Yellowthroats (*Geothlypis trichas*), Ovenbirds (*Seiurus aurocapillus*), Magnolia Warblers (*Dendroica magnolia*), Tree Sparrows (*Spizella arborea*), and Swamp Sparrows (*Melospiza georgiana*). There were, in all, 24 different species of wood warblers, including rarities like Orange-crowned Warblers (*Vermivora celata*), Cape May Warblers (*Dendroica tigrina*), and Connecticut Warblers (*Oporornis agilis*), plus twelve species of sparrows.

Also included were species not normally associated with downtown Toronto even as migrants, such as Yellow-breasted Chat (*Icteria virens*), Virginia Rail (*Rallus limicola*), White-winged Crossbill (*Loxia leucoptera*), Grasshopper Sparrow (*Ammodramus savannarum*), and Long-billed Marsh Wren (*Telmatodytes palustris*). ⌒

WHIP-POOR-WILL

HIGH-RISE HAZARD

Many of Canada's tallest buildings constitute a very real hazard to night-flying migratory birds. Buildings illuminated at night appear to have a blinding or dazzling effect on small, low-flying birds. Night-flying birds usually migrate below cloud-cover and are most likely to strike buildings and other obstacles.

The Toronto-Dominion Centre and adjoining Royal Trust Tower have been notorious culprits in this regard. According to research figures provided by Toronto ornithologists Red Mason and R. Barry Ranford, between the months of September and November 1970 the Toronto-Dominion Centre, then Toronto's tallest building, was the cause of death of no fewer than 375 birds. And from September 8, 1967, until the beginning of spring 1971, 845 birds representing 69 species were picked up at the base of the building or in the shrubbery.

Spring migration casualties were not fully determined but from available infor-

The Black Bear (*Ursus americanus*) isn't only black. It may be yellowish, silvery, tan, or cinnamon. On the islands off the coast of British Columbia, there is a type of North American Black Bear that is creamy white.

COMMON RACCOONS

NOVEMBER

CITY-DWELLING ANIMAL

For the most part man's progress and the expansion of his environment in the form of large towns and cities has caused the lowering of numbers and even complete extinction of many of our native animals.

Not so for the Raccoon (*Procyon lotor*), however. This masked bandit, with its shrewd ways and human-like hands, has learned well to adapt to man's mode of living and even uses him to its own advantage.

According to Dr. Doug Clarke, formerly of the Ontario Ministry of Natural Resources, the raccoon may be as common at present as it has ever been within modern times. Not so with some other city-dwelling animals like the Striped Skunk (*Mephitis mephitis*) and the Red Fox (*Vulpes vulpes*), both of which have declined somewhat in numbers over the past 25 years or so.

Many people report seeing raccoons during the summer months but seldom in winter, and assume, quite naturally, that they hibernate throughout the winter like bears. There is no truth in this, for even when the weather is extremely severe, or when snow-storms blow, they do not actually hibernate. They do sleep for periods during the winter. Often milder weather will encourage them to come out of their temporary hiding places. Then they will go either in search of food, or just to see what is going on in the world. By nature the raccoon is both hungry and inquisitive. At times like this they may be found raiding your garbage cans, garage or tool shed.

1

Winter feeding for birds can commence.

2

Blue Racer (*Coluber constrictor foxi*) measuring 6 feet 3 inches (190 cm) taken at Point Pelee, Ontario, 1915. Record

Atlantic **Giant Squid** (*Architeuthis longimaxus*) captured in Tickle Bay, Newfoundland (55 feet/17 m long overall and weight of more than 2,500 lbs./1,134 kg), 1878.

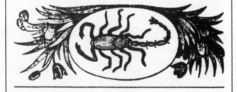

CALENDAR

11

Black Phoebe (*Sayornis nigricans*) reported for Canada (Vancouver, B.C.), 1936.

13

Record **African Elephant** (*Loxodonta africana*) shot in southwestern Angola (12 feet 9 inches/389 cm at shoulder and weight of approx. 24,000 lbs./10,886 kg), 1955.

14

Longest-lived dog, "Bluey", was put to sleep in his home in Victoria, Australia (29 years & 5 months old), 1939.

17

250,000 **Red-winged Blackbirds** (*Agelaius phoeniceus*) seen at Point Pelee, Ontario, 1949.

28

Longest-lived cat, "Puss", died in Devon, England, one day after his 36th birthday, 1939.

The raccoon's favourite hiding place, which also suits as a den, is inside a hollow tree lined with rotting wood. The decaying wood oxidizes and gives off a certain heat which raises the temperature of the den and makes the conditions more comfortable for the animal.

Since raccoons are largely night-prowlers, they are more likely to be observed during the hours of darkness. In fact their eyes often give them away as they are reflected in the headlights of your car.

Not everyone likes the raccoon. Many farmers think it is a pest, for it may raid their henhouses at night. The little bandit is also likely to help itself to the farmer's corn patch, as it is especially fond of corn. In its favour, however, it is charming and friendly, gets rid of a number of insects, and eats lots of garbage. Many persons who are paid regular visits by raccoons are not always happy with this last habit, for the garbage-hunting animals often leave the place looking like a disaster area.

As it is intelligent and highly adaptable, the raccoon is likely to make a very good pet. Humane Societies have them upon occasion. I do not recommend trying to tame an animal captured in the wild, unless perhaps you find it very young or orphaned. If you already have a dog, it is best to forget the idea of having a raccoon for a pet for they are generally very wary of dogs and avoid them whenever possible.

There is one thing I feel you should know about raccoons. One of its favourite foods is fish. If you happen to keep goldfish, or even tropical fish, you may have to choose between fish and the raccoon as a pet.

HIGHEST I.Q.?

As well as being one of our most successful wild animals, the raccoon may well be the most intelligent of North American animals.

There are numerous accounts of raccoons unscrewing complicated tops off bird-feeders, unhooking garbage-can tops, opening barn and garage doors, and removing the suet from a tight mesh bag suspended from a fragile limb without breaking the limb or tearing the mesh.

Dr. K.L. Michels of Purdue University testifies that they learn even more quickly than marmosets and cats. Using food as the key, a number of demanding

high-intelligence tests were conducted on raccoons. It was discovered that they took just 800 trials to achieve 75 per cent success on a given problem. In order to attain the raccoons' peak of accuracy, marmosets required 5,000 trials, and cats needed 7,000 tests to reach the same success ratio. ∞

HIBERNATION THE WINTER SLEEP OF ANIMALS

Winter is a difficult time for most wild animals. Man provides warm shelters, and stores food for himself and his domestic animals, but wild creatures must protect themselves from cold and provide their own food.

Although a few bird species remain with us throughout the winter, most of them migrate. With the approach of cold weather, they use their wings to take them to warmer regions farther south. But those animals without wings must meet the problems of winter as best they can.

Many mammals that inhabit cold climates are active throughout the win-

STRIPED SKUNK

ter, while others enter into a kind of sleep and are not seen again until spring. Such animals are said to hibernate (from the Latin "hibernare", meaning to pass the winter). If an animal in total hibernation is taken from its wintering place, it is found to be cold and stiff, and may appear to be dead. On closer examination, however, it will be found to be breathing, but at a very slow rate.

Most hibernating animals do not remain in such total hibernation. They lie for part of the time in a partial stupor, but occasionally rouse themselves, and are at this time warm to the touch. They may even wake up completely, and emerge from their winter den to take food and drink before retiring again for another period of hibernation.

Some of the few mammals that are

AMERICAN BLACK BEAR

known to hibernate in Canada include the woodchuck or groundhog, the jumping mouse, the chipmunk, the skunk, and the black bear.

The Groundhog (*Marmota monax*) hibernates in a deep underground burrow, where it enters hibernation slowly in a process extending over several days. When in total hibernation, its heartbeat is reduced to 1/20th (5 per cent) of normal, its breathing to 1/25th (4 per cent) of normal, and its temperature falls as low as 5° or 6°F (-15 or -14°C). Waking from hibernation is far more rapid than entering hibernation, and may occur if the animal is disturbed to any extent. The breathing, heartbeat, and temperature all rise rapidly, and within a few hours the animal is fully awake.

There is an old belief that groundhogs come out of their burrows on February 2nd, and if they see their shadows they go back to sleep. This belief has no scientific foundation in fact. Groundhogs are

occasionally seen abroad in January during unseasonably mild weather, but most of them do not emerge until March. In the western mountains lives a counterpart of the groundhog known as the Hoary Marmot (*Marmota caligata*). The marmots living near the foot of the mountains retire earlier than those inhabiting the high, colder areas. The time of entering into hibernation is probably decided less by the effects of temperature than by the physical state of the animal. Marmots do not hibernate until they have accumulated a store of fat.

The Meadow Jumping Mouse (*Zapus hudsonius*) hibernates in a leaf-lined nest about two or three feet (60 or 90 cm) underground. This mouse is perhaps our most complete hibernator, as it enters into hibernation in the fall with the onset of cooler weather and does not reappear until the warm days of spring.

The Chipmunk (*Tamias sp.*) retires into its burrow to hibernate, but some

CHIPMUNKS

BEAVERS CONSTRUCTING A DAM

WOODCHUCKS

doubt exists as to the completeness of its sleep. Unlike most hibernating creatures, the chipmunk stores up quantities of food in its burrow in readiness for the long, cold winter. It is probable that the animal is awake and active some of the time while the rest of the winter is spent asleep, in partial or complete hibernation. In southern Ontario, it is not unusual to see chipmunks above ground during the milder days of the winter.

Although most bat species leave for the south when the weather turns cold, a few remain behind to seek shelter in caves and buildings where they are protected from frost. There they hibernate by hanging by their hind legs, head down. They may roost singly, in small groups, or in tightly packed clusters of hundreds of animals. From time to time hibernating bats rouse and flutter about their refuge, then crowd together again to continue their sleep.

Skunks (*Mephitis mephitis*) den up for the winter in deep underground burrows, while Raccoons (*Procyon lotor*) prefer hollow trees. Both appear to be light sleepers and awaken easily, for they usually emerge quite a few times during the course of the winter.

The Black Bear (*Ursus americanus*) has long been considered as the ideal example of a hibernating animal, although this appears to be somewhat of a misconception. It is doubtful if a bear ever hibernates completely in the manner of the groundhog and the chipmunk. A bear will usually use a cave, a hollow log, or claw itself a space under an upturned root for its winter quarters. Also bears may simply lie down under a tree and there pass into a hibernating stupor. If disturbed, bears may leave their winter quarters and seek a new den, and, like most hibernating animals, are likely to awaken a few times before finally emerging in the spring.

Many non-hibernating animals such as the Beaver (*Castor canadensis*), and the Red Squirrel (*Tamiasciurus hudsonicus*), store up winter food supplies. The beaver stores pieces of poplar and other trees, while the red squirrel stores nuts and seeds in hollow trees or logs. Squirrels often have several such storehouses. Both species are active throughout the winter, although they may stay in their nests for long periods when the winter is unusually cold.

If we ponder for a moment the winter habits of all of these species, we can see that there is not much difference between the animals that hibernate and the ones that don't. The hibernating animals spend most of the winter in sleep and are active for only short periods, while non-hibernating animals are active most of the winter and only remain for short periods of time in their nests. Whereas non-hibernating animals store up food for the winter, most hibernating animals do not. However, hibernators consume extra food before the onset of winter and store it in their bodies in the form of fat.

They draw on this reserve of fat until they begin to eat again in the spring. The chipmunk, usually regarded as a hibernator, stores food in its winter retreat.

Reptiles and amphibians also pass the winter in an inactive state; snakes go underground and turtles and frogs take shelter in mud at the bottom of ponds, or beneath moss and leaves in the woods. These creatures differ from mammals in that they are "cold blooded", which means that their blood is the same temperature as the air or water around them. In summer when the atmosphere is warm, their bodies are also warm. But when the weather gets cooler in the autumn their bodies are so cold they are unable to move. Before they get this cold, reptiles and amphibians retire to places where they are not exposed to the elements, and there pass the winter in an inactive state until the warm weather returns in the spring.

SQUIRREL

Mammals and birds, being "warm blooded", are able to regulate their own temperature, which makes it possible for them to be active throughout the year. Mammals that hibernate, however, are behaving somewhat like reptiles, in that the temperature of their bodies in the winter falls far below their summer temperatures. ✿

B Bear. b

INSECTS IN HIBERNATION

Hibernation occurs in temperate or extremely cold areas where the temperature becomes so low that normal activities of insects are impossible. When the temperature falls appreciably, the majority of insects go into hibernation. The exceptions are the migratory insects like the Monarch Butterfly (*Danaus plexippus*) that travel southward to avoid unfavourable weather conditions. Other insects have modified their habits to a semi-dormant existence.

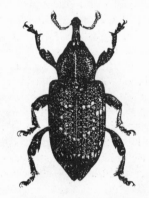

COTTON BOLL WEEVIL

Insects hibernate in all stages of development. Some hibernate as eggs, some as young larvae, full-grown larvae, pupae, or adults. Insects will seek out any sheltered and safe retreat to spend the winter months. The soil is an ideal place for hibernation since insects can descend below the frost line or at least below the line of critical temperature, and are safe from most predators. When moisture exists in the soil, the temperature of the surrounding area rises and gives added protection against frost.

Low temperatures are without doubt the all-important element in inducing hibernation. The Cotton Boll Weevil (*Anthonomus grandis*) begins to hibernate when the mean temperature reaches 55°F (13°C). Many insects, however, go into hibernation before the cold weather sets in. The larvae of the Oriental Fruit Moth (*Laspeyresia molesta*) may begin to go into hibernation in mid-summer. As a matter of fact, they are then in a state of estivation (when all normal activities stop due to extreme high temperatures) until fall when they go into hibernation. The Clover Leaf Weevil (*Anthonomous sp.*) hibernates in the larval, pupal, or adult stage, as with all related groups of this insect.

Perhaps the best-known and most striking form of insect hibernation is the case of the giant Silk Moths (*Saturniidae*). The larvae of these large moths spin thick cocoons around themselves, usually wrapped in a leaf or two and attached to their respective food trees, where they remain throughout the winter months. The thickness of the silken cocoon gives adequate protection against frost, but alas, not always from the beaks of hungry birds, and the attentions of parasitic wasps.

The cocoons of the Polyphemus and the Cecropia are perhaps those most commonly seen in most areas of Canada. Often the Polyphemus cocoon may fall to the ground from its attachment, while that of the Cecropia is especially noticeable as it is attached lengthwise to a twig, and is the largest cocoon of all the insects. ∽

SEED WEEVIL

IT PREYS ON PORCUPINES

The Fisher (*Martes pennanti*), a large species of weasel, has a distinction which no other meat-eating animal has: it is the only creature that habitually dines on Porcupine (*Erethizon dorsatum*).

Its method is to flip the spiny rodent over on its back and attack the unprotected belly. The rodent is dispatched and the fisher settles down to its meal.

Very often fishers have been observed with porcupine quills imbedded in their fur, but they appear to create little inconvenience and they generally work their way free in time. Neither do they seem to cause the terrible festering wounds which are suffered by other animals. ∽

CANADIAN PORCUPINE

FISHER

ℰ THE OTTER DOES NOT MIND THE WINTER ℰ

Perhaps the animal that is least bothered by winter's deep freeze is the Otter (*Lutra canadensis*). This animal, the largest of the weasels, moves about a good deal on land, but has webbed feet and is more at home in the water.

Almost all other animals have to change their way of life in winter: they must eat different food, work harder, and often travel farther in order to stay alive. But not the otter! The otter follows its year-round hunting trails as usual. It can always find a soft spot in the ice where it goes down into the water, often swimming a long way and popping up through another hole. Below the ice it finds the same kind of food as in summer, and it doesn't mind coming out of the water to lie in the snow and eat a fish or a frog when the temperature is below zero.

The winter holds no terror for this rather lovable animal. In fact, it really seems to enjoy the snow, rolling around in it just for fun and sliding along. ↬

⤳ UNPOPULAR IMMIGRANTS ↫

Perhaps the most abundant of our resident birds that overwinter in southern Canada are the European House Sparrow (*Passer domesticus*) and the Starling (*Sturnus vulgaris*). Neither species is native to this country but both were introduced on this continent towards the latter part of the last century.

The house sparrow was the first to be introduced, and from the beginning spread rapidly. Its current occupation had been successfully completed within forty years of its introduction. The earliest records inform us that eight pairs of house sparrows were brought to the Brooklyn Institute from England and released in 1950. This and a number of further experiments failed. In 1854, however, they were introduced to Portland, Maine, where they began to thrive and multiply.

The first Canadian introduction was in Quebec in 1865. By 1870 the house sparrow was noted in Ottawa and by 1875 several colonies of sparrows were established in the Eastern Provinces.

Being largely a grain-eating bird, the house sparrow travelled extensively from place to place along the highways, where it could pick up grain dropped by horse-drawn vehicles. It also fed extensively on semi-digested grain found in horse droppings. The advent of motor vehicles brought a noted decrease in the numbers of these birds in the towns and cities, as they were consequently forced away from the highways into the surrounding rural and suburban regions.

The house sparrow is never found far from human habitation and cultivated lands on which it depends largely for food, and is almost completely absent in the far north. It is, however, reported from Churchill, Manitoba, because of the presence of grain fields in the area. At present, the northern breeding limit of the house sparrow corresponds roughly with the east-west course of the Canadian National Railway, which broadly coincides with the limit of cultivation.

The starling is more tolerant of northern conditions and has been reported about 200 miles (322 km) south of the Barren Ground country.

After several attempts to introduce this bird, the starling was eventually successfully introduced into Central Park, New York, in 1890 and 1891. For the following six years it was wholly confined to the limits of greater New York: little over half a century later it had reached the Pacific coast.

The starling reached Canada first at Brockville, Ontario, in 1919, and by 1925 it was breeding in Ottawa and had arrived in Nova Scotia. In January 1947 a flock of eight birds wandered up the Okanagan Valley to Oliver in British Columbia.

Both starlings and house sparrows are noisy, aggressive birds, and have been the cause of the moving out and decreasing of some of our more desirable native birds that use tree cavities as nesting sites. The Eastern Bluebird (*Sialia sialis*), in particular, has suffered from this intervention. The decrease in the population of the Red-headed Woodpecker (*Melanerpes erythrocephalus*) since the 1920s is very likely due to the deposing habits of the starling. The Common Flicker (*Colaptes auratus*) has also been victimized, for the starling shows a distinct predilection for woodpecker cavities.

However, the excessive wrath and unpopularity that these immigrant birds incur is often unwarranted. These birds do have better sides to their nature. The starling can be considered beneficial, for it consumes large quantities of noxious insects; less than half its food consumption is vegetable and only a small proportion of this is cultivated fruit. It is often blamed for eating cultivated crops when the culprits are usually Red-winged Blackbirds (*Agelaius phoeniceus*) and Grackles (*Quiscalus quiscula*).

In defence of the house sparrow, it can be said that they often share nesting quarters with other birds and live together in peaceful coexistence.

Most frequently, they will occupy the lower level of Purple Martin (*Progue subis*) houses, and surprisingly, will even build their nests inside the much larger nests of hawks. Particular cases on record concern the Osprey (*Pandion haliaetus*) and Swainson's Hawk (*Buteo swainsoni*). They do not appear to interfere with the martins, neither do they show any fear of the large hawks. ↬

CANADA LYNX

DECEMBER

Eleven species and subspecies of mammals and birds are known to have become extinct in Canada since 1844. Many more currently stand on the threshold and can only be saved by the strictest conservation measures. Human encroachment with subsequent habitat destruction and modification has been the major cause of wildlife extinction in this country. In many cases, however, hunting pressure has hastened the process.

The Great Auk (*Penguinus impennis*), which bred widely throughout the north Atlantic and beyond, has the distinction of being the first recorded Canadian species to become extinct in modern times. This large (three feet/91 cm tall), flightless, black and white bird

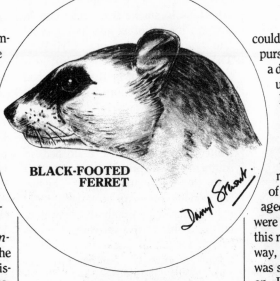

BLACK-FOOTED FERRET

Darryl Stewart

EXTINCT SPECIES IN CANADA

could swim so swiftly it could avoid all pursuers. Unfortunately, on land it was a different story, where it was slow and ungainly and easily approached. Fishermen raided auk colonies and killed the birds for their meat. The slaughter probably commenced with the Vikings prior to 100 A.D. and continued through to the mid-nineteenth century. The destruction of these birds was also greatly encouraged by many museum directors who were desirous of obtaining specimens of this rare bird for their collections. In this way, the death knell for the Great Auk was sounded on Eldey Island off Iceland on June 3, 1844, when the last two remaining birds were killed and the last egg was smashed.

The Passenger Pigeon (*Ectopistes*

3

A **Red & Green Amazon Parrot** was allegedly hatched in captivity in Liverpool, England, and lived for 104 years in the same cage, 1870.

7

Last authenticated **Black-footed Ferret** (*Mustela nigripes*) sighting for Canada (Climax, Saskatchewan), 1937.

8

Highest price paid for a turkey (£1,800) by Tom Granby of Liverpool, England, at an auction at the Waldorf Hotel, London, 1979.

CALENDAR

11

Heaviest brain of any living animal, a male **Sperm Whale** (*Physeter macrocephalus*), taken on a Japanese factory ship in the Antarctic (20.24 lbs./9.2 kg), 1949.

15

Overwintering **Yellow-bellied Sapsucker** (*Sphyrapicus varius*) in Canada (Port Credit, Ontario), 1968.

20

Baikal Teal (*Anas formosa*) in Canada (immature male from Ladner, B.C.), 1957. **Lesser Black-backed Gull** (*Larus fuscus*) at Port Weller, Ontario, 1968.

22

Rediscovery of the **Coelacanth** (off East London, South Africa), 1938.

24

European Jacksnipe (*Lymnocryptes minimus*) in Canada (Makkovik Bay, Labrador), 1927.

27

Charles Darwin sets sail on *The Beagle* for South America and the Galapagos Islands, 1831.

29

An authenticated report of a wolf attack on a human (possibly the only one) near Poulin, Ontario, 1942.

22-28

Christmas Bird Count (founded by Frank Chapman in 1900).

GREAT AUK

migratorius) was probably the most abundant bird to have ever lived; in its heyday it numbered between five and nine billion individuals. Indiscriminate hunting of these birds for "pigeon pie" and the destruction of their habitat were the reasons for their demise. The last passenger pigeon, "Martha", died in the Cincinnati Zoological Gardens on September 1, 1944.

The history of the Labrador Duck (*Camptorhynchus labradorium*) is little known and the reasons for its disappearance are somewhat of a mystery. Its nesting grounds were never discovered but it is assumed to have bred on the Labrador coast. Persecution by man is believed to have led to its speedy extinction, as large numbers of these birds are known to have been killed for their feathers during the mid-eighteenth century. The last authenticated report of a living Labrador duck was made in 1875 from Long Island Sound, New York. Without a doubt, the most beautiful of all the black and white ducks had vanished from the earth.

The Sea Mink (*Mustela macrodon*) was a very obscure animal; little is known about it except that it was greatly valued for its fur. It was redder than the ordinary mink and almost twice as big. It ranged the rugged coasts and offshore islands of Newfoundland, New Brunswick, Nova Scotia, and Maine. The animal was hunted with the aid of dogs; the method used was firing pepper into burrows in which it took refuge, or the application of brimstone to smoke the animal out. In this way the sea mink may have met its fate soon after the American Civil War. The sea mink was first described as a species in 1903, but by that time it had already been extinct for several years.

The Wild Turkey (*Meleagris gallopavo*), which closely resembles our barnyard turkey, still exists in parts of the United States. It once flourished in southern Ontario prior to the destruction of the eastern deciduous forests. The turkey populations were at times greatly reduced during unusually severe winters but were able to recover while suitable habitat remained. The combination of habitat destruction, hunting pressure, and losses during severe winters undoubtedly brought about their disappearance in Canada. In 1962 and 1969, three pairs of turkeys from Virginia were reintroduced into Claremont, Ontario, but after some initial success failed to obtain a permanent foothold there.

Unfortunately, the range of the Eastern Elk (*Cervus canadensis canadensis*) coincided with that of the deciduous forest areas that were settled and cleared for agriculture. This smaller and more richly coloured race of the familiar Wapiti was to be found in southern Ontario, southern Quebec, and the south shores of the Great Lakes, but all that remains of this animal today are the antlers and other bones which are occasionally found during excavations. The eastern elk is considered to have become extinct in Canada around 1850 due to growing settlement and extensive land clearing.

The Queen Charlotte Island Caribou (*Rangifer tarandus dawsoni*) or Dawson Caribou was found in small numbers on that group of islands from which it takes its name. It is supposed to have been a small form, darker in colour than the barren-ground caribou of the mainland and, unlike most of the other races of caribou, the females were usually antlerless. This animal became extinct about 1935 due to hunting pressure from local fishermen.

Two species of Timber Wolf are also known to have died out in Canada. The Great Plains Wolf (*Canis lupus nubilus*), which was also known as the "Buffalo Wolf", roamed with the vast herds of bison over the great Central Plains of southern Manitoba, Saskatchewan, and Alberta. The combined pressure of hunting, trapping, and poisoning gradually eliminated this race until it finally became extinct in the 1930s.

The Newfoundland Wolf (*Canis lupus beothucus*) was restricted solely to that province, but was never considered to have been overabundant. In colour it was entirely white with a slight tinge of ivory yellow on the head and limbs, but black individuals are believed to have occurred. With the settlement of the island, much injury to cattle was reported, and a price was put on its head. Subsequent extinction of the Newfoundland wolf was proclaimed in the late 1930s.

The Northern Kit Fox (*Vulpes velox hebes*) once ranged from the extreme southeastern part of British Columbia to Manitoba, and south into North and South Dakota and Wyoming. It is now officially regarded as extirpated from Canada; the last official sighting in this country was probably from southern Saskatchewan in 1964. Being very trusting, this attractive little fox was easily trapped and snared as settlers moved into its habitat, and much of its natural cover was either destroyed or altered. In more recent times, the kit fox has suffered by being a common victim of poison put out for rodents and coyotes.

The Black-footed Ferret (*Mustela nigripes*) is largely nocturnal, and, according to the records, was always a rare sight in Canada. This largest of the true weasels formerly inhabited prairie-dog towns in southern Alberta and southern Saskatchewan in Canada. In the United States it was found on the Great Plains from Montana to Texas and Arizona, and to 10,500 feet (3,200 m) up in the Rockies. Its stronghold in recent times would appear to be in South Dakota. This animal is closely associated with prairie dogs and may depend entirely on them for its existence by preying on them or using their burrows for shelter. The destruction of prairie-dog towns through poison campaigns has drastically reduced the black-footed ferret to the point where it is now officially regarded as extirpated in Canada. ෴

❝ Only humans are wild. **❞**
Jack Miner

ENDANGERED SPECIES

With man's increasing population and technological progress has come the destruction of the natural habitats of many animals. Man has polluted the air, land, and water; he has logged the forests and drained the wetlands. By this means he reduced some of the rarest, most beautiful, most superbly adapted species of our wildlife heritage to the brink of extinction; these species constitute a resource that could be enjoyed and harvested by sportsmen under good management practices.

Some species have been driven past the point of no return and are lost to us forever. Canada has managed to retain far more of its native wildlife than its neighbour to the south. The contiguous United States has, unfortunately, lost almost all its wolves, grizzly bears, and bald eagles.

Nevertheless, a number of native creatures have been irrevocably lost to Canada within the past century due to man's ignorance and greed. The once abundant Passenger Pigeon, Great Auk, and Great Plains wolf will never grace our land again. Many other species currently stand at the threshold of oblivion and can only be saved by the strictest conservation measures.

In 1970, a list of 92 endangered species was compiled by research biologists of the Canadian Wildlife Services and National Museums of Canada, and was originally published in the *Canadian Field Naturalist* (January –March 1970).

Currently, 33 Canadian species have been assigned formal status by the Committee on the Status of Endangered Wildlife in Canada. Doubtless more species will be added in due course.

CASPIAN TERN

RARE
Birds: Trumpeter Swan, Caspian Tern, Peregrine Falcon -subsp. *pealei*. *Mammals*: Black-tailed Prairie Dog, Plains Pocket Gopher, Grey Fox, Eastern Mole. *Fish*: Speckled Dace, Short-nosed Sturgeon, Giant Stickleback.

THREATENED
Birds: White Pelican, Peregrine Falcon-subsp. *tundrius*, Piping Plover, Burrowing Owl, Ferruginous Hawk. *Mammals*: Peary Caribou.

ENDANGERED
Birds: Peregrine Falcon-subsp. *anatum*, Greater Prairie Chicken, Whooping Crane, Eskimo Curlew, Kirtland's Warbler. *Mammals*: Vancouver Island Marmot, Sea Otter, Eastern Cougar, Wood Bison, Right Whale, Bowhead Whale. *Plants*: Furbish Lousewort.

EXTIRPATED
Mammals: Black-footed Ferret, Northern Kit Fox.

APPROVED DEFINITIONS

RARE
Any indigenous species of fauna or flora that, because of its biological characteristics, or because it occurs at the fringe of its range, or for some reason exists in low numbers or in very restricted areas in Canada but is not a threatened species.

THREATENED
Any indigenous species of fauna or flora that is likely to become endangered in Canada if the factors affecting its vulnerability do not become reversed.

ENDANGERED
Any indigenous species of fauna or flora whose existence in Canada is threatened with immediate extinction through all or a significant portion of its range, owing to the action of man.

EXTIRPATED
Any indigenous species of fauna or flora no longer existing in Canada in the wild but existing elsewhere.

EXTINCT
Any species of fauna or flora formerly indigenous to Canada but no longer existing anywhere. ↩

WHALE SLAUGHTER

Whales are fascinating creatures whose existence has intrigued scientists, artists, and writers for centuries. There are approximately a hundred species of whales in the entire world, including the smaller whales, dolphins, and porpoises, although it is not known for sure just how many species are to be found in the waters off Canada.

Among the most intelligent of animals, whales can communicate with each other by creating a series of high-pitched noises which sound like singing. This can be heard in open waters more than 200 miles (322 km) away.

Whales are also the largest creatures now on earth; in fact the largest species, the Blue Whale (*Balaenoptera musculus*), is the largest animal that has ever lived, exceeding even the largest dinosaurs. A large specimen may attain a length of 100 feet (30 m) and a weight of up to 160 tons (145,150 kg), heavier than 2,000 people. Its heart alone weighs 1,200 pounds (544 kg) and its tongue a third of a ton (302 kg). Newborn calves weigh 2 tons (1,814 kg) and are about 25 feet (8 m) long.

All eight species of great whales have become rare and endangered due to relentless hunting by man. Each year tens of thousands of whales are slaughtered needlessly, by a handful of nations who refuse to abandon the dead-end whaling industry, ignoring the ten-year moratorium unanimously recommended by the United Nations Conference of the Environment.

Unfortunately, the modern whaling

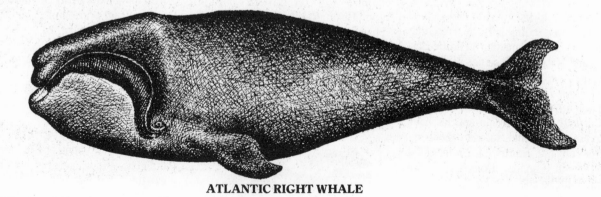

ATLANTIC RIGHT WHALE

industry is big business. Huge convoys of ships roam the seas surrounding Antarctica searching for whales. These fleets are equipped with sonar helicopters, long-range explosive harpoons, and factory ships which can reduce an 80-foot (24 m) whale to nothing in less than an hour.

Whaling has to be one of the cruelest and most barbaric of all hunting activities. The whale is killed by a 200-pound (91 kg), six-foot-long (183 cm) iron harpoon which is shot from a cannon. The harpoon head contains a time-fuse grenade which, literally, blows the whale's entrails apart seconds after impact. The animal may spend hours in agony, and more than one harpoon may be necessary to kill it.

The senselessness of this operation can be shown by the fact that whale slaughter continues to provide products for which there are ready substitutes. Whales are killed for animal feed, industrial oils, fertilizer, perfume, soap, shampoo, gelatin, and margarine, to name just a few. Every one of these whale by-products can be substituted for with substances that are inexpensive and in good supply.

The rate of the killing of these giant mammals during the past ten years has been positively alarming. On the average one whale is killed every thirteen minutes — over 100 every day. In 1976 alone, almost 40,000 whales were killed throughout the world.

The species of whales found in Canadian waters that are of particular concern are: Blue Whale (*Balaenoptera musculus*), Fin Whale (*Balaenoptera physalus*), Minke Whale (*Balaenoptera acutorostrata*), Humpback Whale (*Megaptera novaeangeliae*), Right Whale (*Balaena glacialis*), and Bottlenose Whale (*Hyperoodon ampullatus*).

Those persons wishing to put a halt to this senseless slaughter should voice their support by writing to any or all of the following organizations:

ORGANIZATIONS FOR SAVE THE WHALES

Canadian Nature Federation,
Attn: President and Dr. R. Pratt,
Environment Specialist,
75 Albert Street,
Ottawa, Ontario
K1P 5E7

Canadian Wildlife Federation,
Attn: Mr. Kenneth Brynaert,
Executive Secretary,
1673 Carling Avenue,
Ottawa, Ontario
K2A 2G8

Canadian Federation of
Humane Societies,
Attn: Mr. N.R. Jotham,
Executive Director,
101 Champagne Avenue,
Ottawa, Ontario
K1S 4P3

Greenpeace Foundation,
Attn: Patrick Moore, President, and
Michael M'Gonigle,
2623 West Fourth Avenue,
Vancouver, British Columbia
V6K 1P8

Fisheries Council of Canada,
Attn: Mr. Kenneth Campbell,
Suite 603, 77 Metcalfe Street,
Ottawa, Ontario
K1P 5L6

Newfoundland Fishermen, Food &
Allied Workers' Union,
Attn: Mr. Richard Cashin,
P.O. Box 5158,
King Geo. V Institute,
Water Street,
St. John's, Newfoundland
A1C 5V5

Committee for Original
People's Entitlement,
Attn: Mr. Sam Raddi, President
P.O. Box 2000,
Inuvik, Northwest Territories
X0E 0T0

Inuit Tapirisat of Canada,
Attn: Mr. Eric Tagoona, President
176 Gloucester Street, 3rd floor
Ottawa, Ontario
K2P 0A6

Canadian Council on Animal Care,
Attn: Dr. H.C. Rowsell,
Executive Director,
151 Slater Street,
Ottawa, Ontario
K1P 5H3

Animal Defense League,
Attn: Mr. P.J. Hyde,
38 Fuller Street,
Ottawa, Ontario
K1Y 3R8

World Wildlife Fund (Canada),
Attn: Mr. M. Hummel,
60 St. Clair Avenue East,
Suite 201,
Toronto, Ontario
M4T 1N5 ∾

COMMON FIN WHALE

BOHEMIAN WAXWING

FOR THE PROTECTION OF BIRDS

North American birds have the good fortune to be protected by an international law, which developed from a Convention between Canada and the United States in 1916. The resulting "Migratory Birds Convention Act" (1917) is administered by the Canadian Wildlife Service at Ottawa and applies to the whole of Canada.

In this Act, birds are divided into the categories: Migratory Game Birds, Migratory Insectivorous Birds, and Migratory Non-Game Birds. The first two divisions are self-explanatory, and the last applies to such birds as gulls, herons, and loons.

For obvious reasons non-migratory birds could not be included in an international agreement, but the few there are come under provincial or state governments, as in the case of the Ruffed Grouse (*Bonasa umbellus*). Insectivorous birds that are only partly migratory, such as

chickadees and woodpeckers, are protected by the Act, in which they are given specific mention, and just to make sure that no bird is forgotten, the Act says "and all other perching birds which feed entirely or chiefly on insects".

This makes it sometimes very difficult to give an exact answer to whether a certain bird is protected, but it was probably left that way on purpose to allow some flexibility. It is also flexible in that allowance is made for variations of the game laws in different parts of the country, but these must all be set within the general framework of the Act.

It should also be emphasized that the Act not only prohibits the killing of birds, but also "chasing, pursuing, worrying, following after, stalking, trapping, buying, selling or having in possession". Even a too persistent birdwatcher might be caught on a technicality.

CHRISTMAS BIRD COUNT

Most birdwatchers get their first chance to make a contribution to science by taking part in a bird census. For birdwatchers, the chief census is probably the annual Christmas Bird Count.

The Christmas Count was started in 1900 by the famous ornithologist Frank M. Chapman as a substitute for the "Christmas Hunt", then a favourite holiday pastime. The popularity of this Christmas census has greatly exceeded early expectations and it is now operating in virtually every state and province in North America and Mexico.

The immediate purpose of the census is to count every bird to be found within a given area on one day within a ten-day period that includes Christmas and New Year's Day. In some areas 100 persons now participate. The entire area is divided into sectors and teams of persons are assigned to comb it thoroughly.

In the Toronto area many birds seldom seen in winter have been reported during this count: Virginia Rail (*Rallus limicola*), Northern Shoveler (*Anas clypeata*), Gadwall (*Anas strepera*), American Widgeon (*Anas americana*), Rusty Blackbird (*Euphagus carolinus*), Red-headed Woodpecker (*Melanerpes erythrocephalus*), Pileated Woodpecker (*Dryocopus pileatus*), Oregon Junco (*Junco hyemalis*) (now regarded as a form of Dark-eyed Junco), Black-backed Three-toed Woodpecker (*Picoides arcticus*), Northern Shrike (*Lanius excubitor*), and Winter Wren (*Troglodytes troglodytes*).

The scientific results of the Christmas census have been noteworthy. The data that are obtained permits scientists to study bird-population trends and their relation to changes in habitat, environment, weather, climate, and man's changes in the environment. First evidence of significant decreases or increases are often revealed by the Christmas Count, as are extensions and contractions of range. ∽

❧TROUBLE ON OILY WATERS❧

Thousands of gallons of oily discharge from engine wastes are left each year to float on the surface of the ocean. Oil spreads rapidly and it takes less than a week to cover an area larger than an acre. Sea birds alighting or surfacing in the oily film after a protracted dive are doomed.

Even a minute amount of oil absorbed into their feathers destroys their insulating value by causing them to mat together and interferes drastically with the birds' ability to fly and dive. They thus suffer a slow and miserable death from starvation.

According to the Canadian Wildlife Service, a spot of oil the size of a quarter on the belly of a murre is sufficient to kill the bird.

Murres and eiders are especially high on the list of casualties from oil pollution. They spend much of their time following the currents and fishing on the surface of the ocean. These birds drift with the arctic packs on the southward currents early in the year. During the winter they congregate in the bays and estuaries close to land which are fouled by oil slicks and tar-like blobs on the sea's surface. Riding the ocean currents,

EIDER DUCK

the oil travels for hundreds of miles extending the damage done by the occasional disaster caused through the sinking of an oil tanker.

In the tropical waters dangers from oil pollution would perhaps have less significance. Ocean currents near the great ship lanes between the Old and New Worlds make fish at the surface available to the sea birds in the extreme cold waters.∽

CANADA GOOSE

99

POLAR BEAR PROVINCIAL PARK

Named after one of its outstanding inhabitants, Polar Bear Provincial Park is situated on the shores of James and Hudson bays, approximately 250 miles (402 km) north of Moosonee in northern Ontario. This 9,300-square-mile (24,087 km²) area was formally established in 1970 to preserve one of the truly unique parts of the country. The park includes a significant area of one of the south-ernmost extensions of the arctic tundra in the world, and it supports many species of flora and fauna unique to that region. So fragile is this environment which comes alive with the blooming of myriads of arctic flowers each year, that man's footprints across the lichened rock can remain visible for years.

In the area near Cape Henrietta Maria, the Polar Bears (*Ursus maritimus*) come ashore to their traditional denning areas to bear their young. Apart from the polar bears, other arctic animals such as the Bearded Seal (*Erignathus barbatus*), Walrus (*Odobenus rosmarus*), and Arctic Fox (*Alopex lagopus*) live in the park. Woodland Caribou (*Rangifer tarandus*) are fairly common throughout the area and the Beluga or White Whale (*Delphinapterus leucas*) can often be seen in the river estuaries. The area supports one of the most important breeding colonies of Snow Geese (*Chen caerulescens*).

The park is representative of both the temperate regions of the south and the sub-Arctic regions farther north. Breakup of sea ice comes late and pack ice may drift about off the shores of Hudson Bay as late as August. Summers are short and vary from agreeably warm to disagreeably cold. On warm days the blackflies and mosquitoes can be extremely thick; on cold days, winter underwear and parkas are needed. With its marine coastline characterized by extensive mud flats that are exposed by receding tides, raincoats, sturdy waterproof boots, and hip waders are essential for walking along the coast.

Far removed from human settlement, the park can only be reached by small aircraft. Even then, the frequent and unpredictable sea fog that engulfs the land to a distance of several miles presents a very grave problem. Travelling along its dangerous coastline should not be attempted without suitable boats and competent local Indian guides who are familiar with the coastal conditions.

All provisions and equipment sufficient for survival in the park must be carried and advance enquiries to northern stores concerning the availability of supplies and transportation are essential.

The park, classified as primitive, will be kept in its natural state as much as possible. This park is not for the casual visitor but rather for the highly experienced outdoorsman or scientific researcher.

APPENDIX

CLASSIFICATION OF VERTEBRATE ANIMALS

This classification system is widely used and is one of many types available to the student:

SUBPHYLUM VERTEBRATA — VERTEBRATES

Class Agnatha— Jawless Vertebrates
Class Placodermi— Placoderms (Extinct)
Class Chondrichthyes— Cartilage Fishes (Sharks, Rays)
Class Osteichthyes— Bony Fishes
Class Amphibia— Amphibians
Class Reptilia— Reptiles
Class Aves— Birds
Class Mammalia— Mammals
   SUBCLASS PROTHOTHERIA — MARSUPIALS
   SUBCLASS EUTHERIA — PLACENTAL MAMMALS
      Order Insectivora — Moles, Shrews, and others
      Order Dermoptera — Flying Lemurs
      Order Chiroptera — Bats
      Order Primates — Monkeys, Apes, Man
      Order Endentata — Sloths, Anteaters, Armadillos
      Order Pholidota
      Order Lagomorpha — Rabbits, Hares
      Order Rodentia — Rodents
      Order Cetacea — Whales, Dolphins, Porpoises
      Order Carnivora — Carnivores
      Order Tubulidentata — Aardvarks
      Order Proboscidea — Elephants
      Order Hyracoides — Coneys or Rock Rabbits
      Order Sirenia — Sea Cows (Manatees, Dugongs)
      Order Perissodactyla — Odd-toed Ungulates (Horses, Rhinoceroses)
      Order Artiodactyla — Even-toed Ungulates (Cows, Deer, Pigs)

CLASSIFICATION OF INVERTEBRATE ANIMALS

This list comprises the Arthropods frequently seen on land or in fresh water:

Class Crustacea— Crustaceans
>Order Branchiopoda — Fairy Shrimps, Water-Fleas
>Order Copepoda — Copepods
>Order Ostracoda — Ostracods
>Order Amphipoda — Beach-Fleas, Sand-Fleas
>Order Isopoda — Sowbugs, Pillbugs
>Order Decapoda — Lobsters, Crayfish, Crabs, Shrimps

Class Diplopoda— Millipedes
Class Chilopoda— Centipedes
Class Symphyla— Symphilids (rarely seen)
Class Tardigrada— Water-Bears, Tardigrades (rarely seen)
Class Arachnida— Spiders
>Order Scorpionida — Scorpions
>Order Chelonethida — Pseudoscorpions
>Order Phalangida — Harvestmen, Daddy-Longlegs
>Order Acarina — Mites, Ticks, Chiggers
>Order Araneida — Spiders, Tarantulas

Class Insecta— Insects
>Order Thysanura — Bristletails, Silverfish, Firebrats
>Order Collembola — Springtails, Snowfleas
>Order Ephemeroptera — Mayflies
>Order Odonata — Dragonflies, Damselflies
>Order Orthoptera —Grasshoppers, Locusts, Katydids, Crickets, Mantids, Walking Sticks, Cockroaches
>Order Isoptera — Termites
>Order Plecoptera — Stoneflies
>Order Dermaptera — Earwigs
>Order Psocoptera — Psocids, Booklice, Barlice (Corrodentia)
>Order Mallophaga — Chewing Lice, Biting Lice
>Order Anoplura — Sucking Lice
>Order Thysanoptera — Thrips
>Order Hemiptera —True Bugs, Water Striders, Water Scorpions, Back Swimmers, Water Boatmen
>Order Homoptera —Cicadas, Froghoppers, Treehoppers, Leafhoppers, Aphids, Plant-lice, Whiteflies, Scale Insects
>Order Neuroptera — Lacewings, Ant Lions, Dobsonflies, Alderflies
>Order Coleoptera — Beetles, Weevils
>Order Strepsiptera — Twisted-winged Insects (rarely seen)
>Order Mecoptera — Scorpionflies
>Order Trichoptera — Caddisflies
>Order Lepidoptera — Butterflies, Moths, Skippers
>Order Diptera — True Flies, Midges, Mosquitoes, Gnats, Sheepticks
>Order Siphonaptera — Fleas
>Order Hymenoptera —Bees, Ants, Wasps, Hornets, Sawflies, Horntails, Ichneumons, Chalcids, Braconids

Birds

There are 524 species of birds that are known to have occurred in Canada within modern times.

Common Loon
Yellow-billed Loon
Arctic Loon
Red-throated Loon
Red-necked Grebe
Horned Grebe
Eared Grebe
Western Grebe
Pied-billed Grebe
Short-tailed Albatross
Black-footed Albatross
Laysan Albatross
Yellow-nosed Albatross
Northern Fulmar
Cory's Shearwater
Pink-footed Shearwater
Flesh-footed Shearwater
Sooty Shearwater
Short-tailed Shearwater
Manx Shearwater
Scaled Petrel (Accidental)
Little Shearwater
Black-capped Storm Petrel
Fork-tailed Storm Petrel
Harcourt's Storm Petrel
Leach's Storm Petrel
Wilson's Storm Petrel

White-railed Tropicbird
White Pelican
Brown Pelican
Brown Booby
Northern Gannet
Great Cormorant
Double-crested Cormorant
Brandt's Cormorant
Pelagic Cormorant
Anhinga
Magnificent Frigatebird
Great Blue Heron (Incl.
    white phase)
Green Heron
Louisiana Heron
Black-crowned Night Heron
Yellow-crowned Night Heron
Little Blue Heron
Cattle Egret
Great Egret
Snowy Egret
Little Egret (Accidental)
Least Bittern
American Bittern
Wood Duck
Redhead
Ring-necked Duck

Tufted Duck
Canvasback
Greater Scaup
Lesser Scaup
Common Goldeneye
Barrow's Goldeneye
Bufflehead
Oldsquaw
Harlequin Duck
Labrador Duck (Extinct)
Steller's Eider
Common Eider
King Eider
Northern Shoveler
Spectacled Eider
    (Hypothetical)
White-winged Scoter
Surf Scoter
Black Scoter
Ruddy Duck
Hooded Merganser
Common Merganser
Red-breasted Merganser
Smew (Accidental)
Swallow-tailed Kite
    (Accidental)
Turkey Vulture

Black Vulture

Goshawk

Sharp-shinned Hawk

Cooper's Hawk

Red-tailed Hawk

Harlan's Hawk

Red-shouldered Hawk

Broad-winged Hawk

Swainson's Hawk

Ferruginous Hawk

Golden Eagle

Bald Eagle

Marsh Hawk

Osprey

Crested Caracara
  (Accidental)

Gyrfalcon

Prairie Falcon

Peregrine Falcon

Merlin

American Kestrel

Blue Grouse

Spruce Grouse

Ruffed Grouse

Willow Ptarmigan

Rock Ptarmigan

White-tailed Ptarmigan

Greater Prairie Chicken

Sharp-tailed Grouse

Sage Grouse

Bobwhite

California Quail

Mountain Quail

Ring-necked Pheasant

Chukar

Grey Partridge

Wild Turkey (Extirpated)

Whooping Crane

Sandhill Crane

Common Crane (Accidental)

King Rail

Clapper Rail

Virginia Rail

Sora

Yellow Rail

Corncrake (Accidental)

Purple Gallinule

Common Gallinule

European Coot (Accidental)

American Coot

American Oystercatcher

Black Oystercatcher

Lapwing (Accidental)

Ringed Plover

Semipalmated Plover

Piping Plover

Snowy Plover

Wilson's Plover

Killdeer

Mountain Plover

Eurasian Golden Plover
  (Accidental)

American Golden Plover

Black-bellied Plover

Surfbird

Ruddy Turnstone

Black Turnstone

American Woodcock

European Woodcock
  (Accidental)

European Jacksnipe
  (Accidental)

Long-billed Curlew

Whimbrel

Bristle-thighed Curlew
  (Accidental)

Eskimo Curlew

Upland Sandpiper

Spotted Redshank
  (Accidental)

Spotted Sandpiper

Solitary Sandpiper

Wandering Tattler

Willet

Greater Yellowlegs

Lesser Yellowlegs

Red Knot

Purple Sandpiper

Rock Sandpiper

Sharp-tailed Sandpiper

Pectoral Sandpiper

White-rumped Sandpiper

Baird's Sandpiper

Least Sandpiper

Curlew Sandpiper

Dunlin

Short-billed Dowitcher

Long-billed Dowitcher

Stilt Sandpiper

Semipalmated Sandpiper

Buff-breasted Sandpiper

Western Sandpiper

Marbled Godwit

Bar-tailed Godwit
   (Accidental)

Hudsonian Godwit

Black-tailed Godwit
   (Accidental)

Ruff (Accidental)

Sanderling

American Avocet

Black-necked Stilt

Red Phalarope

Wilson's Phalarope

Northern Phalarope

Pomarine Jaeger

Parasitic Jaeger

Long-tailed Jaeger

Skua

Glaucous Gull

Iceland Gull

Glaucous-winged Gull

Great Black-backed Gull

Western Gull

Herring Gull

Thayer's Gull

California Gull

Ring-billed Gull

Mew Gull

Black-headed Gull

Laughing Gull

Franklin's Gull

Bonaparte's Gull

Little Gull

Heermann's Gull

Ivory Gull

Black-legged Kittiwake

Red-legged Kittiwake
   (Accidental)

Ross's Gull

Sabine's Gull

Gull-billed Tern

Forster's Tern

Common Tern

Arctic Tern

Roseate Tern

Sooty Tern (Accidental)

Bridled Tern (Accidental)

Least Tern

Royal Tern (Accidental)

Caspian Tern

Sandwich Tern (Accidental)

Black Tern

Black Skimmer

Great Auk (Extinct)

Razorbill

Common Murre

Thick-billed Murre

Dovekie

Black Guillemot

Pigeon Guillemot

Marbled Murrelet

Ancient Murrelet

Cassin's Auklet

Parakeet Auklet
   (Accidental)

Least Auklet

Rhinoceros Auklet

Horned Puffin

Common Puffin

Tufted Puffin

Band-tailed Pigeon

Rock Dove

White-winged Dove
   (Accidental)

Mourning Dove

Passenger Pigeon (Extinct)

Yellow-billed Cuckoo

Black-billed Cuckoo

Barn Owl

Screech Owl

Flammulated Owl

Great Horned Owl

Snowy Owl

Hawk Owl

Pygmy Owl

Burrowing Owl

Barred Owl

Spotted Owl

Great Grey Owl

Long-eared Owl

Short-eared Owl

Boreal Owl

Saw-whet Owl

Chuck-Will's-Widow

Whip-Poor-Will

Poor-Will

Common Nighthawk

Black Swift

Chimney Swift

Vaux's Swift

White-throated Swift

Ruby-throated
    Hummingbird

Black-chinned
    Hummingbird

Costa's Hummingbird

Rufous Hummingbird

Anna's Hummingbird

Calliope Hummingbird

Belted Kingfisher

Common Flicker

Pileated Woodpecker

Red-bellied Woodpecker

Red-headed Woodpecker

Lewis's Woodpecker

Yellow-bellied Sapsucker

Williamson's Sapsucker

Hairy Woodpecker

Black-backed three-toed
    Woodpecker

Northern three-toed
    Woodpecker

Downy Woodpecker

White-headed Woodpecker

Eastern Kingbird

Grey Kingbird

Western Kingbird

Thick-billed Kingbird
    (Accidental)

Tropical Kingbird
    (Accidental)

Cassin's Kingbird
    (Accidental)

Scissor-tailed Flycatcher

Great-crested Flycatcher

Ash-throated Flycatcher

Eastern Phoebe

Black Phoebe (Accidental)

Say's Phoebe

Yellow-bellied Flycatcher

Acadian Flycatcher

Alder Flycatcher

Least Flycatcher

Willow Flycatcher

Hammond's Flycatcher

Dusky Flycatcher

Western Flycatcher

Eastern Wood Peewee

Western Wood Peewee

Olive-sided Flycatcher

Vermilion Flycatcher
    (Accidental)

Skylark

Horned Lark

Violet-green Swallow

Tree Swallow

Bank Swallow

Rough-winged Swallow

Barn Swallow

Cliff Swallow

Purple Martin

Grey Jay

Blue Jay

Steller's Jay

Black-billed Magpie

Common Raven

Common Crow

Northwestern Crow

Clark's Nutcracker

Black-capped Chickadee

Mountain Chickadee

Grey-headed Chickadee

Boreal Chickadee

Chestnut-backed Chickadee

Tufted Titmouse

Common Bushtit

White-breasted Nuthatch

Red-breasted Nuthatch

Pygmy Nuthatch

Brown Creeper

American Dipper

House Wren

Winter Wren

Bewick's Wren

Carolina Wren

Long-billed Marsh Wren

Short-billed Marsh Wren

Canon Wren
Rock Wren
Mockingbird
Grey Catbird
Brown Thrasher
Sage Thrasher
American Robin
Varied Thrush
Wood Thrush
Hermit Thrush
Swainson's Thrush
Grey-cheeked Thrush
Veery
Fieldfare
Eastern Bluebird
Western Bluebird
Mountain Bluebird
Wheatear
Townsend's Solitaire
Arctic Warbler (Accidental)
Blue-grey Gnatcatcher
Golden-crowned Kinglet
Ruby-crowned Kinglet
White Wagtail
    (Hypothetical)
Yellow Wagtail
Water Pipit (American
    Pipit)
Sprague's Pipit
Bohemian Waxwing
Cedar Waxwing
Northern Shrike

Loggerhead Shrike
Common Starling
Crested Myna
White-eyed Vireo
Hutton's Vireo
Yellow-throated Vireo
Solitary Vireo
Yellow-green Vireo
    (Accidental)
Red-eyed Vireo
Philadelphia Vireo
Warbling Vireo
Black and White Warbler
Worm-eating Warbler
Golden-winged Warbler
Blue-winged Warbler
Tennessee Warbler
Orange-crowned Warbler
Nashville Warbler
Virginia's Warbler
    (Accidental)
Northern Parula Warbler
Yellow Warbler
Magnolia Warbler
Cape May Warbler
Black-throated Blue
    Warbler
Yellow-rumped Warbler
Black-throated Grey
    Warbler
Black-throated Green
    Warbler

Townsend's Warbler
Cerulean Warbler
Blackburnian Warbler
Yellow-throated Warbler
    (Accidental)
Chestnut-sided Warbler
Bay-breasted Warbler
Blackpoll Warbler
Pine Warbler
Kirtland's Warbler
Prairie Warbler
Palm Warbler
Ovenbird
Northern Waterthrush
Louisiana Waterthrush
Kentucky Warbler
Mourning Warbler
Connecticut Warbler
MacGillivray's Warbler
Common Yellowthroat
Yellow-breasted Chat
Hooded Warbler
Wilson's Warbler
Canada Warbler
American Redstart
Painted Redstart
    (Accidental)
House Sparrow
Bobolink
Eastern Meadowlark
Western Meadowlark
Yellow-headed Blackbird

Red-winged Blackbird
Orchard Oriole
Northern Oriole
Rusty Blackbird
Brewer's Blackbird
Common Grackle
Brown-headed Cowbird
Western Tanager
Scarlet Tanager
Summer Tanager
Cardinal
Rose-breasted Grosbeak
Black-headed Grosbeak
Blue Grosbeak
Indigo Bunting
Lazuli Bunting
Dickcissel
Brambling (Accidental)
Evening Grosbeak
Purple Finch
Cassin's Finch
House Finch
Pine Grosbeak
Grey-crowned Rosy Finch
Hoary Redpoll
Common Redpoll
Eurasian Siskin
   (Accidental)
Pine Siskin
American Goldfinch
Lesser Goldfinch
Red Crossbill

White-winged Crossbill
Green-tailed Towhee
Rufous-sided Towhee
Lark Bunting
Savannah Sparrow (Incl.
   Ipswich Sparrow)
Grasshopper Sparrow
Baird's Sparrow
Le Conte's Sparrow
Henslow's Sparrow
Sharp-tailed Sparrow
Seaside Sparrow
Vesper Sparrow
Lark Sparrow
Bachman's Sparrow
Black-throated Sparrow
   (Accidental)
Sage Sparrow
Dark-eyed Junco
Grey-headed Junco
   (Accidental)
Tree Sparrow
Chipping Sparrow
Clay-coloured Sparrow
Brewer's Sparrow
Wood Stork
Glossy Ibis
White Ibis
White-faced Ibis
Mute Swan
Whistling Swan
Barnacle Goose

Trumpeter Swan Canada
   Goose
Emperor Goose
White-fronted Goose
Snow Goose (Incl. blue
   goose)
Ross's Goose
Fulvous Whistling-Duck
Brant
Mallard
Gadwall
Pintail
Common Teal
Green-winged Teal
Baikal Teal
Blue-winged Teal
European Widgeon
American Widgeon
Field Sparrow
Harris's Sparrow
White-crowned Sparrow
Golden-crowned Sparrow
White-throated Sparrow
Fox Sparrow
Lincoln's Sparrow
Swamp Sparrow
Song Sparrow
McCown's Longspur
Lapland Longspur
Smith's Longspur
Chestnut-collared Longspur
Snow Bunting

Bird Air Speed Records

(Level Flight)

	mph	kph
Spine-tailed Swift	106	171
Frigate-bird	95	153
Spur-wing Goose	88	142
Red-breasted Merganser	80+	129
White-rumped Swift	77	124
Canvasback Duck	72	116
Eider Duck	70	113
Teal	68	109
Mallard	65	105
Pintail	65	105
Canada Goose	60	97
Golden Plover	60	97
Peregrine Falcon	60	97
Racing Pigeon	60	97
Quail	57	92
Merlin	55	89
Sandgrouse	55	89
Swan	55	89
Lapwing	50	81
Snow Goose	50	81
Gannet	48	77

Bird Longevity Records

Birds are, on average, longer-lived than mammals. Very few species exceed forty years and reports that they sometimes live for a hundred years or more should be treated with suspicion. The following are some documented bird longevity records:

European Eagle-owl	68+ yrs.	Adalbert's Eagle	44yrs.
Andean Condor	65	Grey Crane	43
Blue Macaw	64	Caracara	42
Great White Heron	60	Chilean Eagle	42
Ostrich	59	Leadbeater's Cockatoo	42
Greater Sulphur-crested Cockatoo	56	Sarus Crane	42
Imperial Eagle	56	White-tailed Sea Eagle	42
Bateleur Eagle	55+	Asiatic White Crane	41
Black Vasaparrot	54	Manchurian Crane	41
White Pelican	52	Rough-billed Pelican	41
Golden Eagle	50	Bare-eyed Cockatoo	40
Golden-naped Parrot	49	King Vulture	40
Grey Parrot	49	Tawny Eagle	40
Australian Crane	47	Western Slender-billed Cockatoo	40

FRESHWATER FISH

The total freshwater fish fauna of Canada consists of 182 species (including the introduced brown trout, carp, goldfish, and tench).

Sea Lamprey
Pacific Lamprey
American Brook Lamprey
Western Brook Lamprey
River Lamprey
Arctic Lamprey
Chestnut Lamprey
Silver Lamprey
Northern Brook Lamprey
Atlantic Sturgeon
Green Sturgeon
Lake Sturgeon
Shortnose Sturgeon
White Sturgeon
Spotted Gar
Longnose Gar
Bowfin
Blueback Herring
American Shad
Alewife
Gizzard Shad
Pink Salmon
Chum Salmon
Coho Salmon
Kokanee (Sockeye Salmon)
Chinook Salmon

Cutthroat Trout
Rainbow Trout
Atlantic Salmon
Brown Trout
Arctic Char
Brook Trout
Dolly Varden
Lake Trout
Longjaw Cisco
Cisco (Lake Herring)
Arctic Cisco
Bloater
Deepwater Cisco
Kiyi
Bering Cisco
Blackfin Cisco
Shortnose Cisco
Least Cisco
Shortjaw Cisco
Lake Whitefish
Broad Whitefish
Atlantic Whitefish
Pygmy Whitefish
Round Whitefish
Mountain Whitefish

Inconnu
Arctic Grayling
Pond Smelt
Rainbow Smelt
Longfin Smelt
Eulachon
Goldeye
Mooneye
Alaska Blackfish
Central Mudminnow
Redfin Pickerel
Grass Pickerel
Northern Pike
Muskellunge
Chain Pickerel
Chiselmouth
Goldfish
Northern Redbelly Dace
Finescale Dace
Redside Dace
Lake Chub
Carp
Cutlips Minnow
Brassy Minnow
Silvery Minnow
Silver Chub

Gravel Chub

Peamouth

Hornyhead Chub

River Chub

Golden Shiner

Pugnose Shiner

Emerald Shiner

Bridle Shiner

River Shiner

Common Shiner

Bigmouth Shiner

Pugnose Minnow

Blackchin Shiner

Blacknose Shiner

Spottail Shiner

Rosyface Shiner

Spotfin Shiner

Sand Shiner

Redfin Shiner

Mimic Shiner

Bluntnose Minnow

Fathead Minnow

Flathead Chub

Northern Squawfish

Blacknose Dace

Longnose Dace

Leopard Dace

Speckled Dace

Redside Shiner

Creek Chub

Fallfish

Pearl Dace

Tench

Quillback

Longnose Sucker

Bridgelip Sucker

White Sucker

Largescale Sucker

Mountain Sucker

Lake Chubsucker

Northern Hog Sucker

Bigmouth Buffalo

Spotted Sucker

Silver Redhorse

River Redhorse

Black Redhorse

Golden Redhorse

Copper Redhorse

Shorthead Redhorse

Greater Redhorse

Black Bullhead

Yellow Bullhead

Brown Bullhead

Channel Catfish

Stonecat

Tadpole Madtom

Brindled Madtom

American Eel

Banded Killifish

Mummichog

Burbot

Atlantic Tomcod

Brook Silverside

Fourspine Stickleback

Brook Stickleback

Threespine Stickleback

Blackspotted Stickleback

Ninespine Stickleback

Trout-perch

White Perch

White Bass

Striped Bass

Rock Bass

Redbreast Sunfish

Green Sunfish

Pumpkinseed

Bluegill

Longear Sunfish

Smallmouth Bass

Largemouth Bass

White Crappie

Black Crappie

Yellow Perch

Sauger

Walleye

Eastern Sand Darter

Greenside Darter

Rainbow Darter

Iowa Darter

Fantail Darter

Least Darter

Johnny Darter

Logperch

Channel Darter

Blackside Darter

River Darter

Freshwater Drum

Coastrange Sculpin

Prickly Sculpin

Mottled Sculpin

Slimy Sculpin

Shorthead Sculpin

Torrent Sculpin

Spoonhead Sculpin

Deepwater Sculpin

REPTILES AND AMPHIBIANS

Reptiles

43 species (61 subspecies) of reptiles occur in Canada, including 24 species (38 subspecies) of snakes, 14 species (17 subspecies) of turtles, and 5 species (6 subspecies) of lizards.

Snakes

Pacific Rubber Boa (Incl. Rocky Mountain subsp.)
Queen Snake
Northern Water Snake (Incl. Lake Erie subsp.)
Northern Brown Snake or DeKay's Snake (Incl. Midland subsp.)
Northern Red-bellied Snake
Northwestern Garter Snake
Wandering Garter Snake (Incl. Puget Sound subsp.)
Western Plains Garter Snake
Butler's Garter Snake
Northern Ribbon Snake
Eastern Garter Snake (Incl. Maritime, Red-sided, Puget Sound Red-sided and Valley subsp.)
Eastern Hognose Snake
Western Hognose Snake
Northern Ringneck Snake
Blue Racer (Incl. Eastern Yellow-bellied & Western Yellow-bellied subsp.)
Eastern Smooth Green Snake (Incl. Western subsp.)
Eastern Fox Snake
Black Rat Snake
Bullsnake (Incl. Great Basin & Pacific Gopher Snake)
Eastern Milk Snake
Sharptail Snake
Eastern Massasauga Rattlesnake
Prairie Rattlesnake (Incl. Northern subsp.)
Timber Rattlesnake (believed extirpated from Canada)

Turtles

Snapping Turtle
Musk Turtle
Spotted Turtle
Northwestern Pond Turtle
Wood Turtle
Blanding's Turtle
Map Turtle
Eastern Painted Turtle (Incl. Midland & Western subsp.)
Eastern Box Turtle
Pacific Green Turtle
Atlantic Ridley Turtle
Atlantic Loggerhead Turtle
Eastern Spiny Softshell Turtle
Atlantic Leatherback Turtle (Incl. Pacific subsp.)

Lizards

Eastern Short-horned Lizard (Incl. Pygmy Horned Lizard)
Five-line Skink
Western Skink
Northern Alligator Lizard
Northern Prairie Skink

Amphibians

37 species (44 subspecies) of amphibians occur in Canada, including 19 species (21 subspecies) of salamanders; 13 species (15 subspecies) of frogs; 5 species (7 subspecies) of toads.

Salamanders

Mudpuppy
Pacific Giant Salamander
British Columbia Salamander
Green Jefferson Salamander
Blue-spotted Salamander
Long-toed Salamander
Spotted Salamander
Tiger Salamander (Eastern, Grey & Blotched Tiger Salamander)
Red-spotted Newt (Incl. Central Newt)
Northern Rough-skinned Newt
Northern Dusky Salamander
Red-backed Salamander
Four-toed Salamander
Western Red-backed Salamander
Oregon Salamander
Northern Spring Salamander
Clouded Salamander
Northern Two-lined Salamander
Brown Salamander
Red Salamander (Accidental)

Frogs

Olympic Tailed Frog (Incl. Rocky Mountain Tailed Frog)
Northern Cricket Frog
Northern Spring Peeper
Pacific Treefrog
Eastern Grey Treefrog
Western Chorus Frog (Incl. Boreal Chorus Frog)
Bullfrog
Green Frog
Mink Frog
Wood Frog
Leopard Frog
Pickerel Frog
Northern Red-legged Frog

Toads

Plains Spadefoot
Boreal Toad
Great Plains Toad
American Toad (Incl. Hudson Bay Toad)
Fowler's Toad (Incl. Dakota Toad)

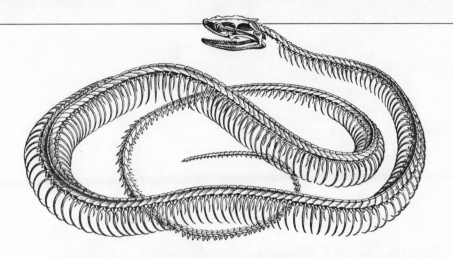

20 of the World's Most Venomous Land Snakes

Australian Brown Snake	Australia
Barba Amarilla	Central and South America
Black Mamba	Africa
Boomslang	Africa
Death Adder	Australia
Gaboon Viper	Africa
Indian Cobra	India and Sri Lanka
Indian Krait	India and Pakistan
Island Viper	Brazil
Jararacussu	South America
Javan Krait	Java
King Cobra	South-East Asia
Many-banded Krait	Burma, China and Taiwan
Mojave Rattlesnake	U.S.A. and Mexico
Puff Adder	Africa
Saw-tailed Viper	Africa and Asia
Taipan	Australia
Tiger Snake	Australia
Tropical Rattlesnake	Central and South America
Yellow Cobra	Africa

RECORD MEASUREMENTS

MARINE MAMMALS

	length		weight	
Blue Whale	109ft.3.5ins.	33m	190 tons*	172,365kg
Fin Whale	90	27	97*	87,997
Sei Whale	72	22	45*	40,823
Sperm Whale	67ft.10ins.	21	72*	65,317
Greenland Whale	67	21	83*	75,296
Humpback Whale	65	20	64*	58,060
Right Whale	60	18	71	64,410
Bryde's Whale	59	17.9	31.5	28,576
Pacific Grey Whale	51	16	39	35,380
Berardius	41	12.5	16.5	14,969
Piked Whale	34	10	9	8,165

*Estimated weight

SHARKS

	length		weight	
Whale Shark	59ft.	1,798cm	90,000lbs.	40,823kg
Basking Shark	45	1,372	32,000	14,515
Great White Shark	37	1,128	24,000	10,886
Greenland Shark	21	640	2,250	1,021
Tiger Shark	20ft.10ins.	635	2,070	939
Hammerhead Shark	18ft.4ins.	559	1,860	844
Thresher Shark	18	549	1,100	499
Six-gill Shark	15ft.5ins.	470	1,300	590
Grey Nurse Shark	14	427	1,225	556
Great Blue Shark	12ft.7ins.	384	550	249
Mako	12	366	1,200	544
Dusky Shark	11ft.11ins.	363	850	386
Whaler Shark	11ft.8ins.	355	768	348
Whitetip Shark	11ft.6ins.	351	750	340
Porbeagle	10	305	500	227
Bull Shark	10	305	400	181

Mammals

192 species of mammals have been known to occur since historic times in Canada or in its coastal waters.

Virginia Opossum

Masked Shrew

Vagrant Shrew

Dusky Shrew

American Water Shrew

Bendire's Shrew

Smoky Shrew

Arctic Shrew

Gaspé Shrew

Trowbridge's Shrew

Pygmy Shrew

Short-tailed Shrew

Least Shrew

American Shrew-Mole

Pacific Coast Mole

Hairy-tailed Mole

Eastern Mole

Star-nosed Mole

Little Brown Bat

Yuma Bat

Keen's Bat

Long-eared Bat

Fringed Bat

Long-legged Bat

California Bat

Small-footed Bat

Silver-haired Bat

Townsend's Big-eared Bat

Eastern Pipistrelle

Big Brown Bat

Evening Bat (Accidental)

Red Bat

Hoary Bat

Pallid Bat

Big free-tailed Bat
  (Accidental)

American Pika

Eastern Cottontail

Nuttall's Cottontail

Snowshoe Hare

Arctic Hare

White-tailed Jack Rabbit

European Hare

Mountain Beaver

Eastern Chipmunk

Least Chipmunk

Yellow Pine Chipmunk

Townsend's Chipmunk

Red-tailed Chipmunk

Woodchuck

Yellow-bellied Marmot

Hoary Marmot

Vancouver Island Marmot

Columbian Ground Squirrel

Richardson's Ground
  Squirrel

Arctic Ground Squirrel

Thirteen-lined Ground
  Squirrel

Franklin's Ground Squirrel

Golden-mantled Ground
  Squirrel

Black-tailed Prairie Dog

Grey Squirrel

Fox Squirrel

American Red Squirrel

Douglas's Squirrel

Southern Flying Squirrel

Northern Flying Squirrel

Northern Pocket Gopher

Plains Pocket Gopher

Olive-backed Pocket Mouse

Great Basin Pocket Mouse

Ord's Kangaroo Rat

American Beaver

Western Harvest Mouse

Deer Mouse

White-footed Mouse

Cascade Deer Mouse

Northern Grasshopper
  Mouse

Sitka Mouse
Bushy-tailed Wood Rat
Northern Red-backed Vole
Gapper's Red-backed Vole
Western Red-backed Vole
Brown Lemming
Southern Bog Lemming
Northern Bog Lemming
Heather Vole
Collared Lemming
Ungava Lemming
Muskrat
Sagebrush Vole
Richardson's Water Vole
Woodland Vole
Singing Vole
Meadow Vole
Montane Vole
Townsend's Vole
Root Vole
Long-tailed Vole
Rock Vole
Chestnut-cheeked Vole
Creeping Vole
Roof Rat
Norway Rat
House Mouse
Pacific Jumping Mouse
Western Jumping Mouse
Meadow Jumping Mouse
Woodland Jumping Mouse
American Porcupine

Coypu
Giant Beaked Whale
Sowerby's Beaked Whale
Blainville's Beaked Whale
True's Beaked Whale
Stejneger's Beaked Whale
Moore's Beaked Whale
Goose-beaked Whale
Northern Bottlenosed
    Whale
Sperm Whale
Pygmy Sperm Whale
White Whale
Narwhal
Blue Dolphin
Common Dolphin
Bottlenosed Dolphin
Northern Right-whale
    Dolphin
White-beaked Dolphin
Atlantic White-sided
    Dolphin
Pacific White-sided Dolphin
Killer Whale
Grey Grampus
Atlantic Pilot Whale
Pacific Pilot Whale
Harbour Porpoise
Dall's Porpoise
Grey Whale
Fin Whale
Sei Whale

Minke Whale
Blue Whale
Humpback Whale
Right Whale
Bowhead Whale
Coyote
Timber Wolf
Arctic Fox
Red Fox
Swift Fox
Grey Fox
American Black Bear
Grizzly Bear
Polar Bear
Raccoon
American Marten
Fisher
Ermine or Stoat
Long-tailed Weasel
Least Weasel
Black-footed Ferret
American Mink
Sea Mink
Wolverine
American Badger
Western Spotted Skunk
Striped Skunk
Canadian Otter
Sea Otter
Cougar
Canada Lynx
Bobcat

Northern Sea Lion

California Sea Lion

Northern Fur Seal

Walrus

Bearded Seal

Grey Seal

Harbour Seal

Ringed Seal

Harp Seal

Hooded Seal

Northern Elephant Seal

Caribou

Mule Deer

White-tailed Deer

Moose

Fallow Deer

Wapiti

Pronghorn

American Bison

Rocky Mountain Goat

Muskox

Bighorn Sheep

Dall's Sheep

Mammalian Speed Records

	mph	kph
Cheetah	63	101
Pronghorn	61+	98
Mongolian Gazelle	55	86
Springbok	52	84
Thomson's Gazelle	50	80
Grant's Gazelle	47	76
European Red Deer	42	68
Black-tailed Deer	40.5	65
California Jack Rabbit	40	64
Cape Hartebeest	40	64
Mountain Zebra	40	64
Blue Wildebeest	37	60
Mongolian Wolf	36	58
Cape Buffalo	35	56
Coyote	35	56

European Rabbit	35	56
Indian Jackal	35	56
Roan Antelope	35	56
American Bison	32	52
Giraffe	32	52
Indian Wild Ass	32	52
Reindeer	32	52
Snowshoe Hare	31	50
American Black Bear	30	48
Guanaco	30	48
Wart-hog	30	48
Black Rhinoceros	28	45
Timber Wolf	28	45
Grey Fox	26	42
African Elephant	24.5	39
Arabian Camel	20	32
Rocky Mountain Goat	20	32
Kouprey	18	29
Asiatic Elephant	16	26
Banteng	11	18
Malayan Tapir	10	16
Rat	6	10
Common Mole	2.5	4
Ai or Three-toed Sloth	0.1	0.2

Maximum Longevity Records in Terrestrial Mammals

Asiatic Elephant	69 yrs.		Tiger	22 yrs.
African Elephant	55		Llama	21
Hippopotamus	54		Common Porcupine	20
Chimpanzee	51+		Common Wombat	19
Short-beaked Spiny Anteater	49		Sumatran Porcupine	18
European Brown Bear	47		Sambar	17
Mandrill	46		Red Kangaroo	16
Lowland Gorilla	40+		Indian Otter	15
Chapman's Zebra	40		Red Fox	14
Brown Capuchin	37		Grey Kangaroo	13
Orangutan	34		Common Marmoset	12
American Bison	33		American Marten	11
Hoolock Gibbon	32+		Golden Marmoset	10
Sumatran Rhinoceros	32		Capybara	9
Malayan Tapir	30		Grey Squirrel	8
African Lion	29		Australian Native Cat	7
Giraffe	28		Coypu	6
Bactrian Camel	27		Algerian Hedgehog	5
Cape Buffalo	26		Lesser Egyptian Gerbil	4
Black Lemur	25		Black Rat	3
Ratel	24		Common Hamster	2
Two-toed Sloth	23		Pygmy Shrew	1

ANIMAL GESTATION PERIODS AND LITTER SIZE

	Gestation	Litter		Gestation	Litter
			Horse	11 months	1
American Bison	270-285 days	1	Kangaroo	38-39 days	1-2
Baboon	6 months	1-2	Lion	108 days	1-4
Black Bear	7 months	1-4	Macaque	160-170 days	1-2
Camel	12-13 months	1	Mink	48-51 days	4-8
Cat	63 days	1-6	Mouse	19-21 days	1-9
Chimpanzee	226 days	1-2	Opossum	12-13 days	4-13
Chinchilla	105-111 days	1-4	Otter	$9\frac{1}{2}$-$12\frac{1}{2}$ months	1-4
Cow	280 days	1-2	Pig	112-115 days	4-6
White-tailed Deer	7 months	2	Rabbit	1 month	1-13
Dog	61 days	1-12	Raccoon	63 days	1-6
Dolphin	9 months	1	Sheep	150 days	1-3
Elephant	21 months	1	Skunk	49 days	4-7
Fox	49-55 days	1-8	Squirrel	44 days	2-5
Gerbil	25-29 days	1-7	Tiger	100-108 days	2-4
Giraffe	14-15 months	1	Wolf	60-63 days	1-13
Gorilla	$8\frac{1}{2}$ months	1	Yak	258 days	1
Hamster	16-19 days	2-12	Zebra	11-12 months	1

GOVERNMENT WILDLIFE AGENCIES

Canadian Wildlife Service,
Environment Canada,
Ottawa, Ontario   K1A 0E7

National Film Board,
Box 6100,
Montreal, P.Q.   H3C 3H5

National Museum of
Natural Sciences,
Ottawa, Ontario   K1A 0M8

Fish & Wildlife Division (Alberta),
Department of Energy &
Natural Resources,
1005 103 Ave.,
Edmonton, Alberta   T5J 0H1

Fish & Wildlife Board
(British Columbia),
Ministry of Environment,
Room 400,
1019 Wharf St.,
Victoria, British Columbia   V8W 2Z1

Wildlife Board (Manitoba),
Department of Mines,
Natural Resources & Environment,
Box 24,
1495 St. James St.,
Winnipeg, Manitoba   R3H 0W9

Fish & Wildlife Branch
(New Brunswick),
349 King Street,
Box 6000,
Fredericton, New Brunswick   E3B 5H1

Wildlife Division (Newfoundland),
Department of Tourism,
Recreation & Culture,
Confederation Bldg.,
St. John's, Newfoundland   A1C 5R8

Director of Wildlife (Nova Scotia),
Department of Lands & Forests,
Box 516,
Kentville, Nova Scotia   B4N 3X3

Wildlife Branch (Ontario),
Outdoor Recreation,
Ministry of Natural Resources,
Queen's Park,
Toronto, Ontario   M7A 1W3

Fish & Wildlife Branch (P.E.I.),
Department of Environment,
Box 2000,
Charlottetown, P.E.I.   C1A 7N8

Dept. of Tourism (Quebec),
Fish & Game,
150, est, boul.,
St-Cyrille, P.Q.   G1R 4Y3

Fisheries & Wildlife Branch
(Saskatchewan), Dept. of Tourism &
Renewable Resources,
1825 Lorne Street,
Regina, Saskatchewan   S4P 3N1

Wildlife Branch (Yukon),
Box 2703,
Whitehorse, Yukon   Y1A 2C6

Supt., Wildlife Service,
N.W.T. Government,
Yellowknife,
Northwest Territories   X1A 2L9

MUSEUMS OF NATURAL HISTORY

Provincial Museum of Alberta,
12845 – 102nd Avenue,
Edmonton, Alberta   T5N 0M6

British Columbia
Provincial Museum,
601 Belleville,
Victoria, British Columbia   V8W 1A1

Manitoba Museum of Man and
Nature/Planetarium,
190 Rupert Avenue,
Winnipeg, Manitoba   R3B 0N2

The New Brunswick Museum,
277 Douglas Avenue,
Saint John, New Brunswick   E2K 1E5

Newfoundland Museum,
Dept. of Tourism,
Duckworth Street,
St. John's, Newfoundland   A1C 1G9

Nova Scotia Museum,
1747 Summer Street,
Halifax, Nova Scotia   B3H 3A6

Royal Ontario Museum,
100 Queen's Park,
Toronto, Ontario   M5S 2C6

Saskatchewan Museum of
Natural History,
Dept. of Culture and Youth,
Wascana Park,
Regina, Saskatchewan   S4S 0B3

NATIONAL PARKS OF CANADA

The National Parks system of Canada was started in 1885 with the setting up of Banff National Park in Alberta. There are currently 28 wildlife reserves under the jurisdiction of Parks Canada:

Parks Canada
(Regional Offices)

Parks Canada,
Historic Properties Bldg.,
Upper Water Street,
Halifax, Nova Scotia   B3J 1S9

Parks Canada,
132 Second Street East,
Box 1359,
Cornwall, Ontario   K6H 5V4

Parks Canada,
C.P. 10275,
Ste-Foy, Québec   G1V 4H5

Parks Canada,
134 11 Avenue, S.E.,
Calgary, Alberta   T2G 0X5

Parks Canada,
114 Garry Street,
Winnipeg, Manitoba   R3G 1G1

National Parks

Auyuitiuq National Park,
Auyuitiuq,
Pangnirtung,
Northwest Territories   X0A 0R0

Banff National Park,
Banff, Alberta   T0L 0C0

Cape Breton Highlands National Park,
Ingonish Beach,
Cape Breton, Nova Scotia   B0C 1L0

Elk Island National Park,
Site 4, R.R. #1,
Fort Saskatchewan, Alberta   T8L 2N7

Forillon National Park,
Box 1220,
Gaspé, Québec   G0C 1R0

Fundy National Park,
Alma, New Brunswick   E0A 1B0

Georgian Bay Islands National Park,
Honey Harbour, Ontario   P0E 1E0

Glacier National Park,
Box 350,
Revelstoke,
British Columbia   V0E 2S0

Gros Morne National Park,
Box 130,
Rocky Harbour,
Bonne Bay, Newfoundland   A0K 4N0

Jasper National Park,
Jasper, Alberta   T0E 1E0

Kejimkujik National Park,
Box 36,
Maitland Bridge, Nova Scotia   B0T 1N0

Kluane National Park,
Mile 1019 Alaska Highway,
Haines Junction,
Yukon Territory   Y0B 1L0

Kootenay National Park,
Box 220,
Radium Hot Springs,
British Columbia   V0A 1G0

Kouchibouguac National Park,
Kent Co.,
New Brunswick   E0A 2A0

La Mauricie National Park,
Box 758,
Shawinigan, Québec   G9N 6V9

Mount Revelstoke National Park,
Box 350,
Revelstoke, British Columbia   V0E 2S0

Nahanni National Park,
Postal Bag 300, Fort Simpson,
Northwest Territories   X0E 0N0

Pacific Rim National Park,
Box 280,
Ucluelet, British Columbia   V0R 3A0

Point Pelee National Park,
Leamington, Ontario   N8H 3H4

Prince Albert National Park,
Box 100,
Waskesiu Lake, Saskatchewan   S0J 2Y0

Prince Edward Island National Park,
Box 487,
Charlottetown, P.E.I.   C1A 7L1

Pukaskwa National Park,
Box 550,
Marathon, Ontario   P0T 2E0

Riding Mountain National Park,
Wasagaming, Manitoba   R0J 2H0

St. Lawrence Islands National Park,
Box 469, R.R. #3,
Mallorytown, Ontario   K0E 1R0

Terra Nova National Park,
Glovertown, Newfoundland   A0G 2L0

Waterton Lakes National Park,
Waterton Park, Alberta   T0K 2M0

Wood Buffalo National Park,
Fort Smith,
Northwest Territories   X0E 0P0

Yoho National Park,
Box 99,
Field, British Columbia   V0A 1G0

For further information regarding National Parks write to:
Information: Director General,
Parks Canada,
Department of Indian and
Northern Affairs,
400 Laurier Avenue West,
Ottawa, Ontario   K1A 0H4

WILDLIFE AND ENVIRONMENTAL ORGANIZATIONS

INTERNATIONAL

Arctic Institute of North America,
2920 – 24 Avenue N.W.,
Calgary, Alberta   T2N 1N4

Arctic International Wildlife
Range Society,
% Dr. Andrew Thompson,
Faculty of Law,
University of British Columbia,
Vancouver, British Columbia   V6T 1W5

Canada-U.S. Environmental Council,
Canadian Nature Federation,
Suite 203,
75 Albert Street,
Ottawa, Ontario   K1P 6G1

Center for International Environment
Information,
300 East 42nd Street,
New York, N.Y. 10017, U.S.A.

The Elsa Wild Animal Appeal of Canada,
P.O. Box 864,
Postal Station K,
Toronto, Ontario   M4P 2H2

The Fund for Animals,
140 West 57th Street,
New York, N.Y. 10019, U.S.A.

Greenpeace Foundation,
2623 W. Fourth Avenue,
Vancouver, British Columbia   V6K 1P8

International Atlantic Salmon
Foundation,
P.O. Box 429,
St. Andrews, New Brunswick   E0G 2X0

International Council for
Bird Preservation,
% British Museum (Natural History),
Cromwell Road,
London S.W.7, England
Canadian Section:
Dr. A. J. Erskine (Secr.),
1215 Agincourt Road,
Ottawa, Ontario   K2C 2H8

International Ecology Society,
1471 Barclay Street,
St. Paul, Minnestoa 55106,
U.S.A.

International Fund for
Animal Welfare Inc.,
P.O. Box 1011,
Fredericton, New Brunswick   E3B 5B4

International Society for the Protection
of Animals,
106 Jermyn Street,
London SW1Y 6EE,
England

International Union for Conservation
of Nature & Natural Resources,
1110 Morges,
Switzerland

International Wildlife Protection
Association,
P.O. Box 728,
Kamloops, British Columbia   V2C 5M4

World Wildlife Fund,
1110 Morges,
Switzerland
Canadian Section:
Director: Monte Hummel
60 St. Clair Avenue East,
Suite 201,
Toronto, Ontario   M4V 1M9

NATIONAL

Alpine Club of Canada,
P.O. Box 1026,
Banff, Alberta   T0L 0C0

Association for the Protection of
Fur-bearing Animals,
1316 East 12th Avenue,
Vancouver, British Columbia   V5N 1Z9

Atlantic Salmon Association,
1405 Peel Street,
Montreal, Quebec   H3A 1S5

Boreal Circle, Boreal Institute for
Northern Studies,
CW 401
Biological Sciences Building,
University of Alberta,
Edmonton, Alberta   T6G 2E9

Canadian Amphibian & Reptile
Conservation Society,
8 Preston Place,
Toronto, Ontario   M4N 2S9

Canadian Arctic Resources Committee,
46 Elgin Street,
Room 11,
Ottawa, Ontario   K1P 5K6

Canadian Association for
Humane Trapping,
% Marietta J. B. Lash
(Executive Secretary),
Box 934,
Station F,
Toronto, Ontario   M4Y 2N9

Canadian Canoe Association,
% Mrs. J. M. Matheson
(Executive Director),
333 River Road,
Vanier, Ontario   K1L 8B9

Canadian Committee for the
International Union for Conservation
of Nature & Natural Resources,
422 Finch Avenue,
Pickering, Ontario   L1V 1H8

Canadian Environmental Law
Association,
Environmental Law Research
Foundation,
1 Spadina Crescent, Suite 303,
Toronto, Ontario   M5S 2J5

Canadian Exploration Group,
P.O. Box 1635,
Peterborough, Ontario   K9H 1G8

Canadian Federation of
Humane Societies,
900 Pinecrest Road,
Ottawa, Ontario   K2B 6B3

Canadian Forestry Association,
185 Somerset Street West,
Suite 203,
Ottawa, Ontario   K2P 0J2

Canadian National Sportsmen's Shows,
Box 168,
Toronto-Dominion Centre,
Toronto, Ontario   M5K 1H8

Canadian Nature Federation,
75 Albert Street,
Suite 203,
Ottawa, Ontario   K1P 6G1

Canadian Parks,
333 River Road,
Vanier, Ontario   K1L 8B9

Canadian Wildlife Federation,
1673 Carling Avenue,
Ottawa, Ontario   K2A 1C4

Canadian Wolf Defenders,
Box 3480,
Station D,
Edmonton, Alberta   T5L 4J3

Consumers' Association of Canada,
251 Laurier Avenue West,
Suite 801,
Ottawa, Ontario   K1P 5Z7

Ducks Unlimited (Canada),
1495 Pembina Highway,
Winnipeg, Manitoba   R3T 2E2

Fisheries Council of Canada,
77 rue Metcalfe Street,
Suite 603,
Ottawa, Ontario   K1P 5L6

Heritage Canada,
P.O. Box 1358,
Station B,
Ottawa, Ontario   K1P 5R4

Maritime Energy Coalition,
Box 1188,
Dalhousie, New Brunswick   E0K 1B0

National & Provincial Parks Association
of Canada,
47 Colborne Street,
Suite 308,
Toronto, Ontario   M5E 1E3

National Survival Institute,
2175 Victoria Park Avenue,
Scarborough, Ontario   M1R 1V6

Outdoors Unlittered,
200 – 1326 Johnston Road,
White Rock,
British Columbia   V4B 3Z2

Acknowledgements
The author wishes to express his appreciation to Warwick L. Nixon for his
valuable assistance. Thanks are also due to Russ James and George Peck of the
Department of Ornithology of the Royal Ontario Museum, Irene Bowman of the
Ontario Ministry of Natural Resources, Oscar G. Rogers, and Patricia Stewart
without whom this book would not have been possible.
Illustrations, other than the author's, are from the following sourcebooks:
Blanche Cirker, ed., *1800 Woodcuts by Thomas Bewick and His School*
(New York: Dover Publications, 1962); Harold H. Hart, ed., *The Animal
Kingdom* (New York: Hart Publishing Company, 1977); Jim Harter, comp.,
Animals (New York: Dover Publications, 1979); Don Rice, ed., *Animals*
(Toronto: Van Nostrand Reinhold, 1979) and *Birds* (Toronto: Van Nostrand
Reinhold, 1980); and J. G. Woods., *The Illustrated Natural History*, 2 vols.
(London: Virtue and Co. Ltd., n.d.).